HOW TO
END THE STORIES
THAT SCREW UP YOUR LIFE

A Step-By-Step Guide to the
Amazing Process of Self-Inquiry

ERNEST HOLM SVENDSEN

Copyright © 2018 by Ernest Holm Svendsen

All rights reserved. No part of this book may be reproduced or transmitted in any form or by any means, electronic or mechanical, including photocopying, recording or by any information storage and retrieval system, without written permission from the author, except for the use of brief quotations in a review.

For more information, contact: ernest@theartofbeinghuman.com

First paperback edition: September 2018

Book design by Ida Fia Svenningsson – idafiasvenningson.se
Illustrations by Charlotte Rosenberg – visualstrategies.io

The Work of Byron Katie and The Judge Your Neighbor Worksheet
are copyright © 2018 by Byron Katie International, Inc. All rights reserved.
Referenced and reprinted here by permission.
www.thework.com

This book is not intended to be a substitute for the medical advice of a professional physician or mental health worker. The reader should consult with their doctor on any matters relating to his/her mental and physical health.

ISBN-13: 978-1724705082
ISBN-10: 1724705083

www.theartofbeinghuman.com

GET THE BUNDLE OF RESOURCES THAT COMES FREE WITH THIS BOOK

- ✓ Ready-to-print versions of the worksheets we will be using

- ✓ A ready-to-print Facilitation Guide (Cheat Sheet)

- ✓ A unique audio session with a guided meditation supporting you to fill out the Judge-Your-Neighbor Worksheet

- ✓ Inspiring audio recordings with real-life examples of people doing Inquiry

- ✓ A Q&A section where I will answer any questions you have around Inquiry

- ✓ Information about online courses and other activities to support you in learning how to do Inquiry

Go to **www.theartofbeinghuman.com/endthestories** now to make sure you have the materials ready when you need them!

I'VE HAD **MANY PROBLEMS** IN MY LIFE.

MOST OF THEM **NEVER HAPPENED.**

CONTENT

11 INTRODUCTION
17 FINDING INQUIRY

31 **PART 1: "YOUR WORLD IS A STORY" – WHY INQUIRY WORKS**
35 THE SIMULATOR
51 THE MAP OF REALITY

69 **PART 2: "CHANGING YOUR MIND" – HOW INQUIRY WORKS**
73 CHANGING YOUR MIND
83 THE WORK OF BYRON KATIE

95 **PART 3: "THE WORK" – HOW TO DO SELF-INQUIRY**
99 IDENTIFY YOUR THOUGHTS
121 IDENTIFY YOUR ONELINERS
127 THE FOUR QUESTIONS
137 THE TURNAROUNDS
157 THE PROCESS AS A WHOLE

163 **BONUS CHAPTER: FINE-TUNING THE PROCESS**

173 APPENDIX A: WORKSHEET EXAMPLES
182 APPENDIX B: EXAMPLES OF DOING THE WORK
192 APPENDIX C: RESOURCES

198 ACKNOWLEDGMENTS
201 SHARE THE LOVE

INTRODUCTION

Your life is a story.

Or more precisely – your life is a *thousand* stories: Stories about your past and future; stories about others and how you relate to them; stories about who you are, and what you can and cannot do.

Some of these stories are great. They bring peace and joy and happiness; they empower you and fill you with kindness and a sense of purpose.

Others are not so great. They hurt. They get in your way. They stop you from doing what you want. They bring limitations, frustrations, stress, fear, sorrow, and pain. And as we shall see, even the great ones can, in fact, get in your way too.

This book is about how to undo those limiting and painful stories. It's a presentation of the power of Inquiry with concrete, step-by-step instructions on how to free yourself from the illusion of your thoughts and return to the effortless joy of simply being present in your life. And I share them, not based on theory or speculation, but from experience.

Walking the Walk

For more than twenty-five years, it's been my privilege to support people in finding freedom from their beliefs. I've worked with individuals from every part of the world and all walks of life. I've worked with former prostitutes, recovering addicts, cancer patients, and people suffering from phobias, burnout, and eating disorders. I've worked with high-level politicians and government officials, award-winning journalists, CEOs in some of the most successful companies in the world, Olympic athletes, popular actors, and star football coaches.

Most of my clients, though, have been completely normal people with completely normal jobs. People who have difficulties in their marriage; who are frustrated with their boss; who want to be better parents; who feel overburdened at work; who find it hard to say no; who are worried about their families, their finances, their career, and their health. Human beings who feel caught in the hamster-wheel of modern life and who want to be in the world in another way – a way that is kinder, more spontaneous, joyful, and sincere.

Over the years, I've conducted hundreds of workshops, in-depth programs, and retreats. I've done thousands of hours of one-on-one sessions with clients, and I've been through rigorous training programs myself, experimenting with many different tools and approaches to working with the mind. What I've found are a number of paths that can take us home to the joyful awareness that I experience to be our true nature.

In this book, I share the essence of one of the simplest, most accessible and effective of these paths in the most concrete and direct way I know how.

Trying to Change the World to Feel Happy

When we're caught in painful stories, we usually react by attempting to change something 'out there.' We try to change the others; we try to change our circumstances; we try to change our boss, our partner, our parents, our children, our body, our wardrobe, our diet, or whatever we think is causing the pain. For many of us, in fact, that is the very purpose of our lives: to make everything just right so we can be happy.

The idea makes perfect sense. If we made more money, found the right home and the right partner, got the kids to behave just the way they should, convinced our aging parent to see the right doctor, got a promotion, lost the excess weight, got a new car, found a better yoga class and a new hairdresser, *then* we would finally be able to enjoy life.

It could be true.

The problem is, it isn't very likely to happen. And even if it miraculously did, it isn't very likely to persist. Sooner or later (and probably sooner rather than later), something would shift. The perfect partner would leave. The aging parent would die. The job would end. The kids would get into trouble. The car would break down. The hairdresser would quit. And we'd be back to square one.

So yes, in theory, it could be true. But in practice, trying to change the world to be happy is a hopeless strategy. In fact, in most cases, it has the exact opposite effect: it makes us miserable. It makes us feel incapable, anxious, and overwhelmed. It makes us stop trusting ourselves, it increases our desire for control, and it sets us up to fail.

Waking Ourselves Up

This book presents another way. A way that addresses the problem at its root. Rather than investing all that energy in the impossible task of trying to fix the world, we can focus directly on the stories themselves.

Because the stories aren't real. They're interpretations. They're constructs in our minds based on a specific view of the world. And whenever this view changes, our stories change as well. And when our stories change – we change.

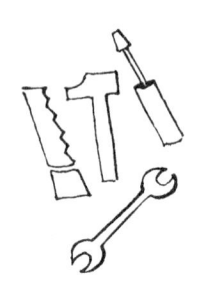

My purpose with this book is to share a concrete set of tools that enable you to wake up when you get caught by your painful or limiting thoughts, to explain exactly why and how they work and to support you as you learn how to use them.

And this is my promise to you: If you apply these tools, they will change your life. I'm not kidding, and I don't say this lightly. The material in this book has the potential to transform your life beyond anything you ever thought possible. I know, both from my own, personal experience, and because I've seen it happen to others more times than I can possibly count.

I have seen people in deep depression; people suffering from burnout; people going through painful breakups; people who have lost children and spouses, jobs and wealth, health and security return to life through this work. And not only return – *expand*. Grow. I've seen them undo their painful stories, throw off their shackles, and step into the river of life alive with love and the courage to overcome their challenges and limitations.

More than that: I have yet to meet someone who wasn't able to apply these tools. Sure – I've met people who didn't *want to* – of course. This work takes a willingness to change, and sometimes, for whatever reason, it's not the right time. But I've never met anyone who sincerely wanted to open their minds and hearts who was not able to. That is the power of Inquiry. It's our birthright. It's available to all. It's as natural as breathing. And once we find it – our lives will never be the same.

Who would you be without your stories? What would it be like to release your painful and limiting thinking about your past and future, about yourself and others, about what you must do, and about what is and isn't possible for you? What would it be like to live from a place of trust and freedom, and to meet the world (and yourself) from there?

The process in this book is the end of your battle with life. It's the doorway to the peace, unconditional joy, and complete inner freedom that is the true aspiration of us all.

There are such things as defining moments. Sometimes they are as simple as turning a page.

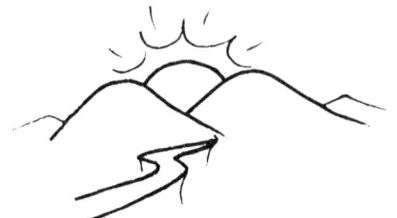

I wish you a beautiful journey.

Ernest.

CHAPTER 1

FINDING INQUIRY

It was just a random sentence. A question that caught my eye on a print-out in a pile of papers.

"What does the thought of 'I' point to?"

Maybe it was the phrasing. Maybe it was the timing. All I know is, I couldn't let it go.

It wasn't that I hadn't considered it before. I imagine everyone asks themselves this question in one form or another now and then: 'Who am I, really?' But this time, it was different. This time, I needed to *know*. Not in theory. Not as a concept or a diagram on a flip-chart. I wanted to know for myself, in my own, personal experience: *Who am I?*

The Voice in My Head

As I began my search for an answer, the first things I discovered were all the things I was *not*.

I was not my body. My body changed all the time and still 'I' remained. I was also not my emotions. Emotions came and went while my sense of 'me' remained uninterrupted. Same with my thoughts. I discovered that I had a voice in my head, which was constantly talking, and in the beginning, I thought that might be me. But as I observed it more closely, I realized that it couldn't be. First, I wasn't in control of it. And second, it was often talking to me as if I were someone else. It would tell me what to do and even attack me at times, scolding me for things I'd done wrong. Most of the time, though, it was just expressing its opinions about everyone and everything while making plans and getting upset when life didn't deliver.

It was the voice that led to my first breakthrough. I was getting really annoyed with it one day because it was repeating a phrase from a song over and over, and I seemed incapable of stopping it, when I suddenly realized that if I wasn't the voice, I had to be the one *listening* to the voice. And with that, it dawned on me, that the closest I could get to 'myself' in this inner extravaganza of thoughts, feelings, images, sensations, daydreams, song-snippets, and imagined conversations was *as the one who was aware of it all*. Every minute, thoughts would come and go. Every day, I would have emotional reactions that would completely evaporate after a few hours. But the one constant was the one who was witnessing all these inner events. I wasn't the voice; I was the one experiencing the voice.

I Am Awareness

I turned my attention toward this inner observer, but it proved to be surprisingly difficult to pin it down. First, there was a problem built into the very act of observing it, since it itself was the one observing. It was like trying to taste my taste buds or seeing how I see.

But there was more to it than that. No matter how hard I tried, I couldn't find a center in this inner awareness. If my thoughts and emotions were psychological objects, this aware consciousness was the space in which they existed. But the space itself was completely empty. There was never any resistance or movement or even boundaries to it. It was just there, allowing everything to come and go, aware of all of it yet completely unaffected.

Then one summer's evening, I was walking along the shores of a lake near my house. There was a light drizzle, and I was considering what the 'it' is, that is raining, when 'it rains.' It seemed to be a trick of grammar that creates this illusion of a 'doer' of the rain. Outside of language, raining is a complete process on its own with no 'it' doing anything.

And that's when it struck me: what if the process of being aware was the same? I had been looking for the subject, the 'it,' the 'me' who was aware. What if there isn't anyone who is aware but there is only awareness itself?

I went inside to check and was overwhelmed with a huge sense of clarity and peace. It was so obvious. Because of my cultural background, I had taken it for granted that there would be a center in there somewhere. That there was a core, a soul, a subject, an 'I.' But there wasn't. In the eye of the storm, there was only a quiet emptiness.

'I' was simply awareness itself.

At Peace

This discovery brought tremendous joy, and I drifted in a sense of inner peace for days. It may sound strange that finding no one at my center would make me happy, but the space of awareness behind all the noise of my thoughts and emotions is the most amazing place. It's home. It's presence. It's peace and clarity and stillness and a sense that everything, just as it is, is entirely and perfectly enough.

I'm sure you know what I'm talking about. I find that everyone has a reference for this experience in their own lives. Times when they have felt the same overwhelming sense of peace and contentment with things exactly the way they are. It's like being filled with a flow of inner sunlight. It's love, really. Inside and out. In my experience, it's who we are. It's our true nature. And it's vast and wonderful. So wonderful, in fact, that once we realize it, there's no way we're ever going to want to leave.

As such, I would love to be able to say that I didn't. I would love to be able to say that I lived happily ever after in this constant state of bliss, always and forever appreciating life in any form it showed up, clearly seeing that since I'm not my thoughts and emotions – since I'm that in which all thoughts and emotions play out – nothing ever bothered me again. Ever.

But alas.

After an initial surge of peace, my apparent problems came back.

The Cycle of Unconsciousness

It wasn't that I ever lost what I had found. Since it wasn't theory for me since I had experienced it directly, my newfound understanding remained within me, and whenever I sat down to relax or meditate, or went for a quiet walk with my dog, I would naturally return to this place of inner peace and awareness. But every time I returned, sooner or later, something would pull me back out. I would become frustrated because something didn't work or I would feel hurt because someone rejected me or some other story would play out, and I would lose myself again.

The cycle was always the same. My mind would be resting peacefully at my center of awareness, and I would be feeling grateful, present, and content. Then some thought would hit me. Often, it would be caused by an outer event, but it could also come up from my memory or as an effect of some other part of the inner flow of my mind. Whatever it was – if I didn't pay attention, it would suck me in. Someone would say 'no' to me, and in a nanosecond, I would be fully identified as 'the rejected one.' Or 'the misunderstood one.' Or 'the disrespected one.' There were so many identities. And the moment I stepped into one of them, that 'me' became my entire world.

It was a lot like being at the movies. As you enter the theater, you are fully conscious of yourself. You find your seat and settle in, you take in your surroundings and the people around you – you're present and aware. Then the movie starts. At first, you're still there, sitting in your seat, watching the screen. But as the movie progresses, your attention is drawn further and further into the action, and in the final scene, when the heroine makes her daring escape along the roof of the speeding train, you have completely forgotten about being at the cinema. You have forgotten about the others, the seats, the screen, the popcorn – your attention is fully drawn into the unfolding story, your emotions responding to the trials of the heroine as she overcomes her challenges and justice eventually prevails. And then: the final kiss and the end credits begin. And you find yourself back in your seat, realizing you really need to use the bathroom and that you have eaten way too much popcorn.

Getting Lost in Stories

I'm sure you recognize this as well. Getting lost in stories seems to be what we humans do.

Take this example. Your doctor has been examining you, and with a concerned expression on his face, he says that he's unsure what to make of your symptoms. There is a risk that it's cancer, but he needs to run some more tests.

What happens?

You're shocked. You have difficulties hearing the rest of what he says. As you drive home, images flash past of you in a hospital bed; you saying goodbye; your family in tears. You cannot focus on the game that night. Your sleep is restless, and you wake up early. Over the weekend, you're distracted and cross. Your stomach is in knots. You experience everything at a distance. You're impatient with the kids. You can't concentrate on your work. You replay the conversation with the doctor over and over in your mind, and when it's finally time to call him for the results, you're so convinced your life is over, you can hardly hear it when he says that everything is fine.

It seems to be an integral part of the human experience to live this way. We do it all the time. In fact, I'll be making the point that most of your life is a story. Or a dream if you prefer the more poetic version. Which wouldn't be a problem if it was a good dream. But it isn't. It's the cause of all the suffering in the world.

EXERCISE: **SUCKED INTO STORIES**

Try this little experiment. Sit down quietly, close your eyes and focus on your breathing. That's all you have to do: simply sit there, eyes closed, with your full attention on this moment, experiencing your breath. In. Out. In. Out. And now see how long you can stay focused in the here and now before your mind travels. It won't be long before you discover yourself replaying a conversation you had earlier today. Or trying to figure out why the heater is making a noise. Or planning your vacation. When you realize that you've travelled somewhere, come back to your breath and try again.

> Before you know it, you're sitting on the swing in your kindergarten playground. Or reliving the argument you had with your daughter last week.
>
> Thoughts come and go all by themselves, and some of them take us with them to far off places in time and space. It is surprisingly difficult to simply stay present and attentive here and now.

Stories are Painful

When you're lost in a story – any story – it will inevitably lead to pain.

With some stories, that's obvious. Take the 'I am seriously ill' story from before, or any of the classics like 'they don't like me' or 'I did it wrong' or 'I need more money.'

With other stories, it's less obvious. The 'I'm a nice person' story, for instance. That would seem like a really good story. It makes us feel all warm and fuzzy inside, and what's wrong with being a nice person? Well, nothing, obviously. Only, if that's our story about ourselves, sooner or later it will get in the way. If nice is who I am, what do I do in the situations when I'm required to be not so nice? When I must say a very clear 'no' to someone or I must let someone off at work, or I can't satisfy the needs of someone who is important to me. When a conflict arises between being perceived as nice and being true to myself, then what?

Stories make us inflexible. Stories get in the way. Because they are never true, sooner or later all stories lead to a conflict with life. And when you are at war with life, you lose.

Looking for a Way Out

So, this was my new world. I had found a deep insight into who I was, but I kept forgetting it and losing myself in the myriads of stories that were playing out all the time. And, I could see that everyone else was the same. When my friends came to me for help or support, I could hear how deeply they were caught in painful concepts. How they were spinning stories from their interpretations of what someone said or did, and how they were absorbed in their dreams of past and future, completely ignoring that they were safe and secure in the present.

As I began looking for ways out of these psychological gravity wells, I remembered that when I was a child, I found a trick to handle scary movies. Whenever I felt too overwhelmed by what was happening, I would think about how the people behind the scenes had made the movie. How the blood wasn't real blood and how there was an entire crew standing around the actors with lights and microphones and cameras, and that would always calm me down. It would take me out of the illusion and bring me back to myself and my surroundings.

I gradually realized that I could do something similar with my inner movies. That they, too, were constructs, crafted by my unconscious to achieve specific goals, and behind the scenes of my conscious mind, a lot was going on to produce and uphold the world I was living in. And, more importantly, I discovered that whenever I peeked past the curtain at the machinery behind, the stories I was so certain were true would dissolve into thin air.

When You Examine the Stories, they Lose Their Hold on You

There were two questions that interested me:

1. How do I get out of a story once I'm in it?
2. And how do I take the energy out of it, so it doesn't suck me back in next time it shows up?

The answer to both questions turned out to be the same. When you deeply examine – not in theory but through your own, direct experience – the elements that go into your stories, they lose their hold on you.

It's like experiencing a magic trick.

Imagine a skilled magician who performs a card trick that completely astounds you. Imagine that he then explains to you in detail how he carries it out, demonstrating how he diverts your attention, and with an elegant sleight of hand swaps one card for another.

And then imagine that he performs the trick for you again.

Will your experience be the same this time?

No.

Because now you understand how he pulls it off. You can appreciate the quality of his performance and the precision of his movements, but you no longer fall for the illusion. Even though he is doing everything *exactly* as before, your insight into what's really going on causes you to have a very different inner experience.

That's how Inquiry works. It's a way of getting your perspective back, of loosening the hold the dream has on your mind by seeing how it's constructed.

The Purpose of This Book is to Help You Discover Through Your Own Experience

I honestly don't know how to express the positive impact the practice of Inquiry has had on my life. Fewer and fewer stories have the power to pull me in, and when they do, I know how to find my way back. The peace and joy this has brought to me are beyond words. And since it's been my business for years now to support others in doing the same, I've been blessed with the privilege of experiencing countless clients and participants go through the same amazing transformation.

In its simple, step-by-step form, the process of Inquiry is life-changing. But only if you do it, of course. The entire point of self-Inquiry is to make *your own* discoveries. As such, my intent with this book is practice. Everything I say is geared toward that one purpose: to show you exactly how to do Inquiry on your own, enabling you to work effectively with your limiting stories and the elements of your thinking that are causing you pain, holding you back, or getting in your way.

To this aim, I will be focusing on a particular form of Inquiry called *The Work of Byron Katie*[1]. I have experimented with many different approaches over the years, and in my experience, this method is by far the best place to start. It is clearly structured, it is relatively simple, it does not require the practitioner to accept any dogmas, and it has been tested and refined by the experiences of tens of thousands of people over more than three decades.

The Journey Ahead

The journey ahead is a simple one, and I've split it into three parts.

In part one, we cover the basics. I will try to show you how this thing you call reality is really your own construction, and that the built-in contradictions and mistaken interpretations that make up this so-called reality are the true causes of whatever stress, pain, and frustration you experience.

In part two, we'll look at what I call your *map of reality*, and how it's the beliefs that make up your map of reality that are the pivotal elements in making any real changes in your life.

And in part three, we'll turn to practice, and I will walk you through a detailed explanation of how to use *The Work* to see through the stories that are moving you away from freedom, joy, and peace.

I can promise you an exciting journey.
With a little luck, in fact, you may well be standing on the threshold of a completely new understanding of your life.

And it begins very simply.

It begins with the most important thing there is to say about anything.

---

[1] *The Work of Byron Katie* and the *Judge-Your-Neighbor Worksheet* are copyright 2018 by Byron Katie International, Inc. All rights reserved. You can read more on www.thework.com.

PART 1

YOUR WORLD IS A STORY
- Why Inquiry Works

WE ARE SUCH STUFF AS DREAMS

ARE MADE ON; AND OUR LITTLE LIFE IS

ROUNDED WITH A SLEEP.

– WILLIAM SHAKESPEARE

The Tempest, Act 4, scene 1

CHAPTER 2

THE SIMULATOR

So. Let me begin by explaining why stories play such an important role in your life. And as promised, let me do it by sharing the most important thing there is to say about anything. First, however, let me make one point: The most important thing there is to say about anything is very simple. So simple, in fact, that it's hard for most people to understand how important it really is when they hear it for the first time.
Or the second.

But here it is:

There is only now.

There is only now. This, right now, is the only thing that exists.

As I said, it's very simple, but it's crucial because it means that anything that isn't now isn't real. It only exists in our thoughts. As stories. As ideas in our minds.

The Future is Imagined

Take the future, for example. Our ability to simulate the future is one of the most important factors in the success of our species. Being able to foresee what will happen, what other people will do and how a situation will unfold is extremely valuable. Whether you're using it to set a bear trap or to orientate yourself in traffic, your ability to imagine the future is such an integral part of your life that you hardly notice it. And you're so good at it that you often believe that what you imagine about the future is real.

But it isn't, of course.

After all, where is the future? Right now, in this moment, as you read these lines, where is it? Where is tomorrow? Where is next year?

The answer is: in your mind. The future only exists as a thought. As images in your internal world, extrapolations from your experiences, simulations of reality as you believe it will unfold. You may think, for instance, that you're going to go to the movies tonight. You have ordered the tickets, you have arranged where to meet your friends – everything is in place. And then the phone rings. Your daughter has been injured at gymnastics, and you end up spending the evening at the emergency room instead.

You were absolutely certain you knew what your future held for you, and yet it changed because what you were so certain of was, in fact, nothing but an idea. It was a simulation, a guess based on the information that was available at the time.

The Past is Gone

Even though we forget it sometimes, very few people find it difficult to see that it must, of course, work like this. That the future doesn't exist 'out there,' but rather, it is present here and now as thoughts in our minds.

It can be a little more challenging to accept that it works the same way with the past. Still, where is the past right now? Where is what you did yesterday? Where is last week? Where is your trip to the kitchen to make tea or the thunderstorm that rolled in over your house half an hour ago? Just like the future, there is only one answer: in your mind. The past isn't *here*. The only thing here is your *memory* of the past – just as it's only what you *imagine* about the future that actually exists. And the format they exist in is also the same: inner simulations in the form of images, sounds, physical sensations, and other sensory experiences.

What's confusing to us about saying that the past is no longer here is that the apparent effects of the past still are. You can remember what you read on the previous pages, ergo, you must have read it. It's wet on the terrace, ergo, it must have rained. The newspaper is on the table, ergo, you must have fetched it from the mailbox outside. And this is all quite correct. There's nothing wrong with your memory. It's simply that although the newspaper is there, the trip to the mailbox isn't. It exists only as a memory – images, sounds, and physical sensations that you are now (re)creating. The situation itself is gone. All that's left are some signal patterns in the nerve cells in your brain. You can simulate the event in your mind. You can recreate part of the sensory signals you experienced when you were outside, and in that way, experience it again. You can do it many times. Just as you can recreate the sound of the thunder in your mind. Maybe you filmed it on your phone so that it's even easier to recreate the details. But it's not real. It's all simulations – patterns in your neural pathways, ones and zeroes in your phone's memory – which only exist in the now.

How Memory Works

There have been numerous studies focusing on the process of how we remember the past, and although there are many things we still don't fully understand about the brain, one point is clear: our memory doesn't function the way most people think it does.

The most common metaphor for memory is that our brains are like recording devices, storing up all the impressions they receive via the different senses, and remembering is equivalent to replaying those recordings like you'd replay a film.[2] But the truth is that it would be far too uneconomical for the brain to store an exact copy of everything we experience. Instead, we store just a few elements – a look, a sound, the color of a sweater, a smell. After that, whenever we want to remember the situation, we do so by recalling these different fragments and use them to reconstruct it – plugging in the gaps with what we think was probably there when it happened. But in fact, what we use to plug the gaps is pure imagination. In other words, only a very small proportion of any given memory is created from stored information. By far the greater part is something we've invented.[3]

The result is that our memory is extremely unreliable.

Take, for example, an experiment conducted at the University of Washington, where a group of test subjects was shown a video of a traffic accident, after which they were asked how quickly they thought the cars were going when they hit each other. Then they were asked whether they had seen any shattered glass in the video. In reality, there wasn't any, but 14% answered that there was, which is entirely to be expected. The interesting thing is that if the first question was formulated in a different way – how quickly were the cars going when they *smashed into* each other – 32% subsequently answered that they had seen shattered glass. This tiny difference, 'hit' versus 'smashed into,' meant that more than twice as many people falsely remembered having seen shattered glass. And people are very sure of themselves in this regard. In a related experiment, a group of adults was shown a manipulated childhood photograph of themselves in a hot-air balloon, and afterward, half of them said they could remember the incident, recounting it in vivid detail, even though it had never taken place.

It's Never Too Late to Have a New Childhood

Your memories of the past aren't lying in some archive deep inside your brain or on a mental hard-disk, ready to be replayed. Your memories are constructions you create afresh each time you 'remember,' and the situation and emotional state you find yourself in *when* you remember have a crucial effect on the contents of that construction.

Say, for example, that you've hosted a party that you experienced as quite successful at the time. But the next day, you receive negative feedback from some of the guests. Suddenly, you'll remember the party in a very different way. Not because anything changed in the past, but because something changed now. Your understanding of the party changed and now you project a different story backward in time.

If we don't understand that time is a story – by which I mean that our past and future only exist as simulations – then we believe that our past is a fixed and objective thing, which has a decisive influence on who we are today. In reality, the opposite is the case: who we are today has a decisive influence on our past. Which is why I like to say that it's never too late to have a new childhood. Your childhood is not what happened in the past. Your childhood is how you perceive it today. Just as your future is how you imagine it at this moment. They are projections in time, stories in your mind. And I know that it may be difficult to take in at this point – and don't worry if it is, it will become clearer as we progress.

But the truth is: your stories aren't real.

They are only thoughts.

EXERCISE: **DO YOU IN FACT HAVE A PROBLEM RIGHT NOW?**

Consider a problem in your life. Something that worries you – a relationship that isn't working or a financial issue or some difficulty at your job.

Now investigate: right now, in this specific moment, as you're reading these lines, is that problem actually present? Does it have any impact on this moment, outside of your thoughts? Is it 'real' right now or does it only exist as a simulation, a story in your mind?

What would it be like if you were able to only deal with your problems when they were relevant instead of carrying them with you into all the other activities of your day?

There is an old story about two monks who were travelling together. They had both made a vow of chastity, and they were keeping silence from day break to sunset. At one point, they arrived at a river where a woman was having problems getting to the other side. The older of the monks saw her difficulties, and as they were passing, he went to her and carried her across the water, where he dropped her off so she could continue on her way. The two monks walked on in silence for the rest of the day, but no sooner had the sun set before the younger of the men spoke up.

'What was that?' he asked accusingly. 'You know we're not supposed to be in contact with women, let alone carry them around. Have you lost your mind?'

The elder monk looked at him calmly and answered.

'I dropped her off at the other side of the river. You have been carrying her around all day.'

There is No Other Place Than Here

It works with space the same way as it does with time. Just as there is no other time than *now*, there is also no other place than *here*.

Let me show you what I mean.

Imagine that it's Monday morning. The alarm clock rings, you get up, eat breakfast, and get ready to go to work. And while you're brushing your teeth, you think about the new watercoolers that have been installed at your office.

What you don't know is that a gas line exploded underneath your office building during the night, razing it to the ground. All that's left is a pile of rubble, and the sparkling new watercoolers have been crushed beyond all recognition. In what we call objective reality, the building no longer exists. But in your thoughts, it's still there, just as it usually is. Because, in fact, it's only a simulation.

Just as other moments in time – besides now – can only exist in your imagination, so can other places besides here. When you're at home, in your bathroom, brushing your teeth, your office and the new watercoolers are made of exactly the same material as your past and future. In that moment, you're only experiencing them in your imagination. Just as you're only imagining the kitchen when you're sitting in the living room considering getting a glass of water. Which is not the same as saying that the kitchen isn't 'there.' It's just that in *your* reality, in *your* subjective experience, which is the only experience you'll ever have, when you're sitting in your living room, the kitchen is just a thought. As is every other place, including your place of work. And when you don't know that your office and the new watercoolers are gone, in your simulation, they're still there. As you're brushing your teeth, you live in a world with watercoolers. And you will continue to do so until someone updates you, and you readjust your simulation.

Your Mind is a Simulator

The future, the past, the places that are not *here* – they're all constructions of thought. The human mind is a simulator, and more than anything else, it's our ability to simulate that which is not, which sets us apart from other animals. It's the secret super-power that has made us rulers of this planet and allowed us to outcompete all other species despite our vast array of physical shortcomings. It's at the core of everything that makes us human and the basis for all our advanced cognitive abilities, including creative thinking and communicating with language.

When, for instance, you hear the word 'elephant', the reason you can understand what it means is that you can simulate an elephant in your mind. You've spent your entire life building up an enormous vocabulary, which means that certain combinations of sounds, on the face of it completely meaningless, are connected to certain very specific images. When you hear the word 'elephant', a picture of an elephant appears in your head. You 'simulate' an elephant in your mind.

It's the same with all other thought processes as well. When a child works out that he can pull a box over to the kitchen table and clamber up onto it to reach the cake plate, he's using his inner simulator. The box has never been over by the kitchen table before, but he's tried climbing on it by the sofa and has discovered that he can use it to get higher. He's already tried standing by the kitchen table and established that he can't reach the plate. In his mind, he now stitches these two experiences together into a completely new simulation – something he hasn't tried yet, which is the possibility of reaching the cake plate by standing on the box – and finds a solution to his problem.

EXERCISE: **THE BUILDING BLOCKS OF YOUR MIND**

Our inner simulator works with representations of reality based on sensory perceptions: sounds, physical sensations, images, smells, and tastes. These are the building blocks that we translate all concepts and ideas into when we work with them. Which isn't necessarily something we notice. Under normal circumstances, you're not aware of the image of the elephant when you hear the word, or of the colors you most likely ascribe to different weekdays to keep them organized in your mind, because most of these processes are unconscious. Our thinking would slow dramatically, and we'd be completely overwhelmed if we were conscious of all that goes on behind the scenes in the everyday activities of our minds.

Our brains are, therefore, split into two: an extremely fast, unconscious part, and a much slower, conscious part, and most people have no notion of the vast number of sensory processes that are actually involved in the unconscious bit whenever we think. But if we slow things down and become more aware, we can catch a glimpse of what's going on in the background. Try, for instance, to explore the way you experience a word like comfort. What is comfort? Close your eyes and work out what comfort means to you. How do you understand it? How do you grasp it with your mind? If you become still and pay attention, you can see the inner images you've woven around the word. Maybe you feel a sensation in your body. Maybe you even experience a color, a sound, or a certain taste.

Now try with another word: success. Explore the way you experience the word success. What is success? Close your eyes and work out how you represent success in your mind. Become still and observe what happens inside you when you focus on the word success. It's another set of images, another physical sensation, another soundtrack.

You Live in an Expanded Reality

Simulating reality is one of the mind's primary functions. It's by simulating the future that you decide what to do next. It's by simulating your childhood that you know who you are. And it's by simulating the kitchen that you know where to go when you're thirsty. Simulating reality is what enables us to experience our world in time and space. It's what enables us to make sense out of anything, and we're constantly using our simulators to expand and interpret our surroundings.

Take this moment, for example. How much of what's going on right now is a simulation? I'm writing this book, but for me, it currently exists only as an idea about the future. I'm sitting in my office, a mental concept that is held together by a multitude of other concepts, all based on different simulations. And while I'm busy with these constructions, I also have a clear idea of what's beyond the walls in this so-called office. I simulate the rest of my house, the garden, the street, my neighbors. I simulate the entire city, the country – the planet, even. And in fact, I need go no further than the edge of my field of vision before my simulations kick in. As soon as I shift my gaze, my simulator takes control of holding my surroundings steady – this is why I'm not surprised when I look back and see that my pen is still lying on the table. I simulate everything I can't see: the armchair behind me, the coffee table, the window. Just as you're simulating them as you read this. Try and take a closer look! What does the armchair look like? It's in there somewhere because that's the only way you can understand what you read.

Here, I just heard a car drive by. Or rather, I believe I heard a car drive by. In reality, I heard a sound, which I *interpreted* to be a car, and then I saw an inner image of a car driving by. But really, it was only a simulation. And now, my gaze falls on a teacup by my hand. I know instantly what it is: my favorite cup. I can feel what it's like to hold it, what it's like to raise it to my mouth, what it's like to drink from it. And at the same time, in my mind, I see my daughter, who's always trying to get hold of it before I do, and I hear her laughter and sense how it feels to fight over it with her. It's much more than just a cup. It's a portal into my inner world, a doorway for my mind, loaded with memory and meaning.

The Cause of All Your Problems

Our whole lives play out in this expanded reality. From your capacity to think to your memories of the past and conceptions of the future, to your ideas about what's happening elsewhere, and even to the way you create meaning in what's going on right now, your simulator is involved. Without it, your world would fall apart.

To verify this, simply consider what would happen if you became unable to simulate anything outside of the present moment. What would happen if you couldn't simulate any past or future or any object, person, or location other than what is present right here, right now?

You would lose everything. You would have no idea who you were, where you came from, where you were going, what you were doing, or what was going on around you. Your ability to simulate the world is crucial. Without it, nothing we call human would make any sense.

It does, however, come at a cost.

Because as necessary as they are, our simulations are anything but neutral. Built into the connections that link the sight of my favorite cup with thoughts about my daughter and the word 'elephant' with the animal is a whole conception of the world. How you define success, the images that show up when you think about your childhood and how you imagine tomorrow, next week, and next year isn't random.

It's based on a unique, underlying structure.

And it is in the mismatch between this structure and reality as it is that the true cause of all your problems can be found.

---

[2] In a 2011 study carried out on 1,500 Americans it emerged that nearly two thirds of those interviewed (63%) believed that memory functions like a video camera, and half of them believed that once memories are established in the brain they remain reliable and unchanging. (D.J. Simmons and C.F. Chabris: *What people believe about how memory works*, PLoS ONE, 2011, 6:8).

[3] How we construct memory is a fascinating topic covered in many works and experiments. Personally, I am very fond of António Damásio's work. Damásio is a Professor of Neuroscience, Psychology and Philosophy at the University of Southern California and he has published several books on the brain. A good place to start is here: António Damásio: *Descartes' Error: Emotion, Reason, and the Human Brain*, Putnam, 1994; revised Penguin edition, 2005.

CHAPTER 3

THE MAP OF REALITY

Imagine a farmer, a real estate agent, and a geologist looking at a field.

Are they seeing the same thing?

No.

They're *looking at* the same thing, but they're not *seeing* the same thing.

The farmer sees some excellent topsoil, where he could plant a lovely crop of wheat. The geologist sees an exciting moraine landscape from the Cretaceous period. And the estate agent sees a piece of land where you could put a stunning villa with a view over the bay. They're *looking* at the same thing, but they're *not seeing* the same thing.

Why not?

Because they have different 'maps of reality.' They have different backgrounds, they have different experiences, they have been exposed to different knowledge, different values, and different perspectives on life and so their nervous systems have been formed in very different ways.

Everyone has Different Maps of Reality

All your experiences, all your knowledge – everything you're exposed to during your life – create particular patterns and structures in your nervous system that are crucial in terms of how your simulator works. These structures are your 'map of reality.' They are the framework within which everything you experience is organized. They are to your thinking what grammar is to language: the backbone of your perception of what's happening and the framework for the actions you think are possible in any given situation.

It's because of differences in our maps of reality that we humans have different goals, different patterns of behavior, different expectations of the future, different memories of the past, and different interpretations of the present. Nobody else simulates reality the way you do. Nobody else responds as you do when they hear the words 'watercooler' or 'kitchen table'. They don't call up the same images. They don't activate the same memories. What you consider comfortable is different from what I consider comfortable. And when you dream about success, those dreams are different from mine. It's my map of reality that connects the teacup to my daughter, and it's in your map of reality that you find material for the armchair you picture in my office.

It's our map of reality that makes us who we think we are. It's our map of reality that is the basis for all our stories about the world. Our ability to operate with unique maps of reality is a key ingredient in our success as a species.

It is also the cause of all our problems; and where to find the solutions.

Let me show you why.

The Process of Evolution is a Process of Adapting

Your ability to create a unique map of reality and use it to orientate yourself in life is the result of a long process of evolution. A process, which in turn, is about adaptation.

Those organisms that respond best to their surroundings have the best chance of survival. And most organisms have spent millions of years to evolve and adapt to their particular environments through specific sets of responses that are stored in their genes. Like the ability of plants to turn toward the sun or the ability of bees to find their way home.

In animals, we call these innate responses 'instincts,' and animals that work only by using instincts can only survive in environments in which their instincts suit. A slug can survive in the woods (and in our villa garden), because it is here, its instincts work. It has no resources to survive elsewhere since it cannot learn or develop new strategies.

Developing a Nervous System that can Learn From its Environment

To overcome this limitation, evolution came up with a new and more advanced type of nervous system that allows organisms to learn from their environments. A dog is a good example of an animal that works in this way. On the one hand, like the slug, a dog is guided by many instincts; but on the other hand, unlike the slug, it can also learn new behavior. That's why we can train our dogs to follow simple commands. But obviously, it's not for our sake that dogs have developed this ability. From an evolutionary point of view, it's about adaptation and survival in unfamiliar environments. And unlike the slug, dogs can adapt to new surroundings. In fact, second to humans, dogs are probably the mammal that has achieved the widest spread on the planet. From the African savannah to the Greenland ice sheet, dogs have found their niches and adapted to life.

But dogs are still limited by their genetic memory, and the flexibility of their brains only go so far. Particularly, dogs are not very good at learning from each other.

So, evolution took another step and developed its biggest success so far: the human nervous system. Our ability to think and learn from our environment enables us to develop unique and complex patterns of behavior and pass them on to new generations in a much faster and far more nuanced way than storing instincts in the genes. And this has led to an unprecedented ability to adapt. There is hardly any environment we humans cannot operate in. Whether we're born into a primitive tribe deep in the Amazon, among Persian merchants at the time of the Roman empire, or in a small apartment in Tokyo in the twenty-first century, we are able to internalize the culture, beliefs, and worldview we grow up around and develop a unique map of reality that is as fundamental to how we operate as innate instincts are to a slug.

Human Beings are Born with a Readiness to be Programmed by Life

Human beings, in other words, are born with a readiness to be programmed by life. We don't have to rely on the slow process of developing and storing instincts in our genes. The plasticity of our brains means that we can adapt to completely new environments. This is our greatest gift. But it's also the cause of all our problems. Because sometimes, the environments we adapt to are not very healthy. Sometimes they are so filled with built-in contradictions that it is literally impossible to adapt successfully to them. And sometimes, once we have adapted to a particular environment, if the conditions change, it takes a while for our map of reality to catch up, and for a time, we become, in effect, like a slug on the beach.

The human mind is an open system. It's extremely sensitive to its environment. If you grow up with a manic-depressive mother, this has a huge impact on the map of reality you develop, and consequently, on how you understand and experience life.

The slug is simple, but it's robust. We are complex and adaptable, but consequently, we're in constant danger of breaking down under our own weight. I don't know this for a fact, but I'm pretty sure that slugs don't get depressed or have separation anxiety. They just live, and then they die.

We are different. Our understanding of our environment is shaped by our experiences, and how we perceive the world is entirely dependent on what is present in our map of reality. As it is the case with the farmer, the geologist, and the real estate agent. None of them are more right or wrong. They simply have different maps of reality and so they perceive and simulate the world very differently.

Your Experience of Life is a Direct Effect of your Map of Reality

Our operating from different maps of reality has an enormous impact on our lives. You can visualize this by imagining that you and I were going to a party, each of us bringing a video camera. Before we go, we agree that you'll film everything fun, enjoyable, and friendly about the party, while I'll film everything that's boring, sad, and unpleasant. We do exactly that, and the next day, we meet to watch our recordings. Will it look like we went to the same party?

No.

Our recordings will feature the same surroundings, of course, and many of the people we filmed will also be the same. But your recording will look like it was made at the world's most amazing party, and mine will look like a recording of every hostess' worst nightmare.

These recordings are like the stories we construct out of the material the world offers us. There are so many things going on inside and around you all the time that you must constantly sort through enormous amounts of information. A completely normal transit or commute ride, for example, offers the opportunity for an almost infinite range of films, depending on how you edit them and what you focus on. And this editing goes on all the time. Your nervous system is constructed to pay attention to things that are important. But what is important? That depends on your preconceptions. It depends on your beliefs. It depends on your map of reality.

Consequently, two people can, in principle, live the same life, but they'll experience it very differently because their maps of reality – and hence, their simulations and the stories they superimpose on the world – lead them to completely dissimilar perceptions of it.

What You Experience isn't Necessarily True

Imagine, for example, a couple who completely agree on one thing: respect is the foundation of every good relationship. If things are going to work, it's crucial that both partners respect each other.

They decide to move in together, living like that for several months, but then they break up, and they move out. And now, she's sitting in a café with her friends shortly afterward and they, of course, ask her what went wrong. And she answers: "Well, we broke up because he simply didn't respect me. Because every time we had a discussion, he would raise his voice and become really loud and use bad words and speak in a harsh tone, and I mean, that's not respectful. If you respect someone, the least you can do is address them in an appropriate tone."

Naturally, her friends agree. There's a significant overlap between their maps of reality – that's why they're her friends.

At the same time, up in the apartment, her now ex-boyfriend is talking to *his* friends, who ask the same question: what went wrong? And he answers: "Well, we broke up because she simply didn't respect me. Because every time we had a discussion, she became totally controlled and reticent, almost polite. And that's not respectful. If you respect someone, the least you can do is trust them enough to honestly express how you feel and let them see where you're at and what you're thinking."

The obvious trick question here is, of course: which of them is in the right? To which, the only response is that both of them are. Or neither if you prefer. The problem is that it entirely depends on what their respective *maps* of reality look like. It depends on how they understand respect. Is it respectful to speak nicely and politely to each other or is it respectful to honestly express your feelings?

In my experience, it's always our maps of reality that are the problem when we disagree about something. In fact, I would go so far as to say that none of the discussions and debates I have ever had with my wife, my children, my colleagues, or my friends are about reality. They're about our different maps of reality. It's the simulations we superimpose on reality, the stories we spin about reality, and the meaning we ascribe to reality that are the true cause of our disagreements, and it's when we overlook that fact that we run into problems.

Your Map of Reality is Based on Beliefs

I call the elements that constitute our map of reality 'beliefs.' In the example about the couple breaking up, the problem is that they have different beliefs about what respect is, and I use the word 'belief' to show that even though it isn't an objective truth, in practice, it's true for us. Just think of all the times when you know intellectually that there might be other interpretations of someone's actions, but your whole nervous and emotional system is so convinced that your interpretation is the right one that you live – and behave – as if it were true.

If you believe that someone is out to get you, it affects how you behave toward them; if you believe that it's 'every man for himself,' you'll show up in a very different way than if you believe that 'we're stronger together,' and if you grow up in a culture where you learn that 'men are superior to women' or that 'children should be seen and not heard,' it may have a huge impact on your life.

Our map of reality and the beliefs that constitute it form the framework that our simulations – and, therefore, our thoughts – operate within. If we describe the process of thinking as moving through a maze, then our beliefs are the walls that determine where our thinking can go. Everybody has a different set of beliefs, which is why our trains of thought are different. There are pathways and openings in one person's maze that do not exist in another's.

Your Beliefs are Self-Reinforcing

One of the key challenges around our beliefs is that they are self-reinforcing.

Since our map of reality is built on our experience, the more experience we have with something, the more certain we are that it's true. But equally, the more times we experience something, the greater the likelihood is that we'll notice it again the next time. This means, that once we've seen something once, we're more apt to notice it a second time, making us even more certain of it, and thus increasing the likelihood of us seeing it yet again, and so on.

If, for example, I'm going to meet a group of people and I've been told beforehand by someone I trust that one of them is one of the nicest people I'll ever encounter, it's very probable that that's exactly what I'll see: I'll notice how calm she is, and how she generously gives everybody else room to express their opinions.

If, on the other hand, she'd been described to me as a nasty woman who's always on the lookout for mistakes and loves to criticize, then that's what I'd see. And I'd be able to confirm that she is sitting there smiling arrogantly, silently noting everyone else's slip-ups.

The point is that her behavior is the same. I'm just interpreting it differently because I'm using what (I think) I know to understand what (I think) I see. And if I believe she's nasty, next time I meet her, I will continue to perceive her along those lines. Because now, of course, I know what she's like, so I can see how she pretends to be friendly on the surface, but–

thankfully – I've seen through her charade, so I don't let myself be taken in.

A Powerful combination of Adaptation and Stability

Your beliefs are constantly being reinforced in this way. If you think there are too many immigrants in your country, then you'll notice all the newspaper articles about problems with immigration. If you think that fears about smoking are exaggerated, then you'll latch onto the stories you hear about people who've smoked their entire lives and never had a day's illness. If you think that public transport is inadequate, then you'll remember all the times when your train was delayed.

This is no accident, of course. On the contrary, this combination of flexibility and stability is a genuinely elegant design on nature's part. On the one hand, as a human being, you have a greater gift for adaptation than any other species that has ever existed. On the other hand, the self-reinforcing nature of the system helps to make it more robust, so you don't have to up sticks and reorganize your entire understanding of reality every time something happens that you didn't expect.

In large-scale terms, it's a brilliant system. It works. But on an individual level, it comes at a cost: you can easily end up stuck in negative patterns of perception that you cannot escape.

Your Map of Reality Gives Meaning to Your World

Your map of reality is important because it creates meaning from the stream of sensory input that is constantly washing over you. It is as if you experience reality through a filter that tells you what everything is, simultaneously allowing you to grasp what's going on but also superimposing layers of information and meaning (see fig. 1).

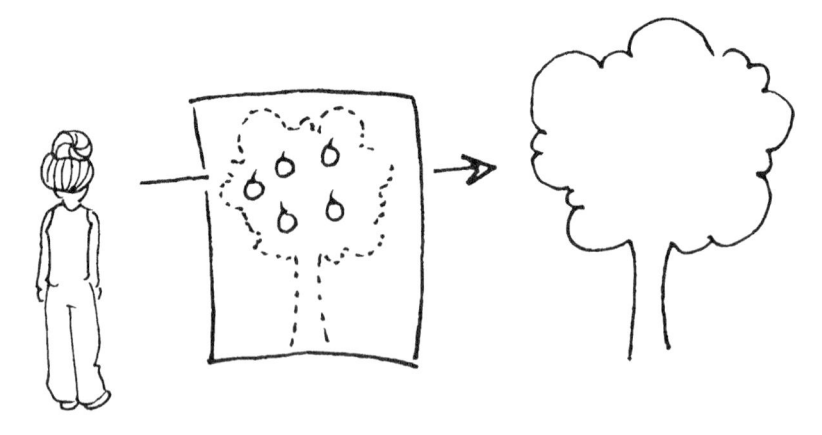

Fig. 1: A filter of meaning
Your Map of Reality is like a filter that exist between you and the world that tells you how to understand and interpret everything that is going on. If you didn't have this filter, your world wouldn't make any sense at all.

If a man comes bursting into your office and starts telling you off, for example, it's by referring to your map of reality that you determine whether he's happy or irritated, angry or sad. And when you've found your answer, that's the story you'll superimpose onto him.

It doesn't feel like *you* are doing anything, of course. It feels self-evident; a simple observation of facts. But obviously, that can't be the case. It takes interpretation to know what a certain type of behavior means, and somebody else with a different set of beliefs in their map of reality wouldn't necessarily perceive him the way you do. Where you see him as angry, they might see him as worried or afraid – or maybe even engaged.

This makes no difference to you, though. As he comes bursting into the room, you experience a man who's speaking angrily to you. And that, therefore, is the reality your body and your emotions are going to respond to.

Your Emotions React to Your Inner Reality

The fact is, your emotions don't react to what's happening *outside* of you. They don't react to what we call 'objective reality' or to 'the truth.' They react to the reality you experience: the reality you create *inside* yourself.

> ### EXERCISE: **REACTING TO INNER REALITY**
>
> Try this little experiment: imagine a lemon. A small, compact, yellow lemon. Imagine its bumpy peel, its pointy ends, and its firmness as you hold it. Now imagine taking a sharp knife and cutting the lemon into halves and then cutting one of those halves into quarters. Imagine looking at its juicy flesh as you pick one of the quarters up, bring it to your mouth and bite into it. Imagine your teeth sinking into the flesh, and the juice running over your tongue. If you take a moment to conjure it up, you'll immediately notice the effect: a tension in your jaw and a change in your production of saliva.

Changing your production of saliva isn't something you have conscious control over. It's not something you can decide to do. If I ask you to increase the amount of alpha-amylase you produce or alter the balance of pepsin in your stomach acid, you'll have no idea what to do. But the moment you simulate what it feels like to bite into a lemon, they occur instantaneously.

Your emotions are the same. They do not respond to external reality. They respond solely to what's happening in your mind. For your emotions, your mind's reality is the only reality. Your emotions only know what's going on in your mind, so to speak. As such, the world's most dangerous snake could be slithering by behind you, and if you don't know it's there, you won't be afraid. Just as it doesn't matter how quietly the dog is sleeping in its basket – if you believe it's going to attack you, you'll be on high alert.

Your Inner Reality is Just a Story

This means that two people can be exposed to precisely the same thing but respond emotionally in two completely different ways, because what they're responding to is, in fact, their *interpretation* of that thing, and not the thing itself.

If, for instance, you're afraid of spiders or enclosed spaces, you'll react completely differently from someone who isn't when you come across a house spider or get stuck in a lift. It's not the spider or the lift *per se* that's frightening. It's your beliefs, the inner stories that are woven around them in your map of reality, and the associated simulations, that scare you. If you're afraid of heights, then it's not the height itself that's scary. It's the images whirring in your inner simulator of what it would be like to fall and get dashed to pieces on the rocks that are making you afraid. Just as my experience of being bitten by a dog as a child can make me afraid of a dog that's sleeping peacefully in its basket today. The past has nothing to do with this particular dog, but the sight of it activates a series of internal images from back then, and they are what's actually frightening me. This is why I can't do anything but react. In fact, there would be something wrong if I *didn't* react. After all, that's what my nervous system is designed to do – to help me adjust to the world I was born into by using my experiences to select the most appropriate response to what's going on around me. So if my experience of dogs is that they are dangerous, it's only natural that I would be afraid when I see one. Even if it's sleeping peacefully.

However irrational they may seem, all your emotional responses – your frustration, your anger, your fear, your joy – are signs that your nervous system is working. They're the body's way of preparing itself to deal with the challenges it thinks lie ahead.

It's Never Reality that is the Problem

If you don't realize that what seems like the 'real world' is, in fact, created by your own inner reality, you will always be beset by a fundamental misunderstanding: believing that the source of your joy and pain exists outside of yourself. If you believe this, you will also believe that the way to solve your problems is to tinker with the world until it fits your story about it. But trying to change reality to solve your problems is like trying to get rid of dirt on a projector lens by cleaning the canvas on which the image is projected.

It doesn't matter how hard you work or how much time you spend – so long as the marks you're trying to remove are actually due to something on the projector, your efforts will be in vain. It's not until you turn your attention to the projector itself that things change.

None of your problems – and I really do mean *none* of your problems – are caused by reality. They're caused by the stories you tell yourself about reality. It's what goes on inside your internal simulator that causes the stress and suffering you feel.

Always.

And please don't misunderstand me here. I'm not saying that since all your problems are caused by your own stories, you should stop acting in the world, become a doormat, and silently accept every injustice and wrongdoing you experience. On the contrary. In my experience, the more stories I've stepped out of, the less I get in my own way, and the more effective I've become in dealing with things. If something doesn't work for me and I don't have a story about it, there's nothing stopping me from taking appropriate action. But there's a huge difference between letting your actions spring from fear, distrust, and confusion, and letting them spring from love, clarity, and kindness. It's simply more effective to act from a clear mind and to invest your energy where it makes sense.

When your children haven't tidied their rooms, is it the mess that's the problem or is it your beliefs about the mess? 'They're irresponsible.' 'They don't respect me.' 'They'll never learn.' Notice all the interior images you see, all your projections of the past and future, all the rules in your map of reality that you feel aren't being kept. They're all just stories. And notice how you approach your children when you believe this.

When your boss criticizes you, is it what he says that's the problem or is it the stories you create? Or when the computer doesn't work properly? Or when your flight is delayed? Or when your project falls through? Or when your team doesn't perform well? Or when the tiles fall off the roof? In themselves, these are all things that simply *are*. They are reality. Tasks to engage with. Work to get done. It's when they're coupled with your inner narrative that they become difficulties, burdens, trouble.

The World is a Rorschach Blot

Your husband walks through the room, and you tell yourself a story about how nice he is. Or how sexy. Or how irritating. But what does that have to do with him? His mother will have a different story about him. His sister will have another. His colleagues at work have theirs. His best friend has his.

Who is right?

Your story about your husband is yours. Just as with everything else in your world, you see him through the filter of your map of reality. Just as with everything else in your world, he's your projection. The only thing that's really going on is that a man is walking through the room. Everything else – *everything* else – is a story you're superimposing on that.

The world simply is. Like a Rorschach blot, it means nothing in itself. It's only when *you* look at it that it begins to resemble something. A disrespectful partner. An unreasonable colleague. A favorite cup.

They're all just stories.

The question is: how do we change them?

PART 2

CHANGING YOUR MIND
- How Inquiry Works

IN THE BEGINNER'S MIND
THERE ARE MANY POSSIBILITIES,
IN THE EXPERT'S THERE ARE FEW.

– SHUNRYU SUZUKI
Prologue, Zen Mind, Beginner's Mind

CHAPTER 4

CHANGING YOUR MIND

During high school, I used to work in a video store. Even though I liked it, I was convinced that my boss didn't think I was doing a good enough job. Every time he was nearby, I got flustered and nervous, trying my very best to do everything right – which, as you can probably predict, only had the effect of making me tense and clumsy.

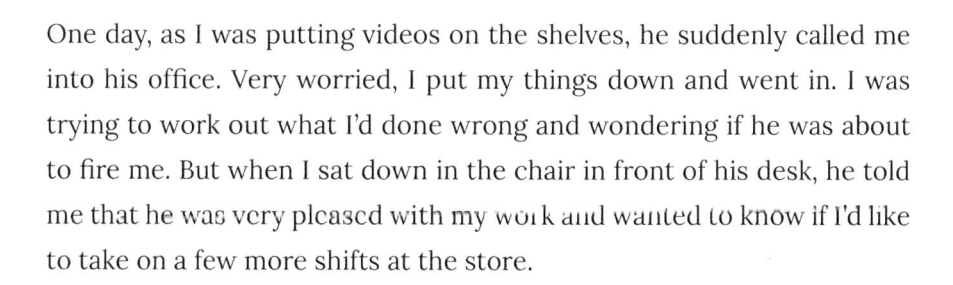

One day, as I was putting videos on the shelves, he suddenly called me into his office. Very worried, I put my things down and went in. I was trying to work out what I'd done wrong and wondering if he was about to fire me. But when I sat down in the chair in front of his desk, he told me that he was very pleased with my work and wanted to know if I'd like to take on a few more shifts at the store.

Before my boss called me into his office, I was a young man putting videos on a shelf. After I'd been in to see him, I was a young man putting videos on a shelf. The situation was *exactly* the same – nothing in the outside world was different. But one moment I was stressed and worried, and the next, I was happy and calm, and the only thing that had changed was what I believed.

We Don't Choose Our Beliefs

Our world is created by our beliefs. It's our beliefs that generate the framework for our thoughts, our actions, and the way we perceive what's going on around us. I don't know, whether what my boss told me that day was true. Maybe he was lying when he said he thought I was doing a good job. Maybe he was just desperate for staff. But *I believed him*, and so my reality shifted. And with that shift came a new sense of certainty and calm, which unlocked exactly those qualities in me, that ended up making me one of the most trusted and appreciated employees in the store.

If I could have pushed my beliefs about my boss' view of me aside earlier, I would have. I tried. I tried to convince myself that I was just being silly. I tried to tell myself that I was imagining things. But it didn't work. Because we can't choose what we believe in. We can't decide for ourselves what to be afraid of or who to fall in love with. If you don't believe in God, you can't just decide to do so. And if you believe your boss doesn't like you, you can't just decide that he probably does. Why? Because our map of reality is shaped by our *experiences*, and experiences reach far more deeply into our nervous system than any number of rational arguments and logical deliberation.

I could have had endless discussions with my friends about whether or not my boss was satisfied with my work. They could have tried a thousand ways to convince me, listing all the good things I'd done, arguing that I was an excellent employee, pointing out one positive thing after another, but it wouldn't have worked. Inside, I would still have been convinced that he was dissatisfied with me, because that was what I thought I experienced whenever he was around. That was how I interpreted his glances, his pauses, his way of giving me instructions. But the moment he himself told me that he was happy, even going so far as to offering me extra shifts, my conviction changed. Because at that moment, I had a new experience that shifted my map of reality.

Your Map of Reality is Shaped by Experience

Your map of reality is created by your experiences. And the only thing that can change your map of reality is new experiences. As I've explained, this offers a challenge, because your map of reality is self-reinforcing: you use the experiences you've already had to understand fresh ones. Once you have begun perceiving a situation in a particular way, this perception becomes part of the filter you use to understand it, so you continue to interpret it in the same way, making it difficult to be rid of the unhelpful beliefs that get lodged in your mind – such as the idea that a particular person doesn't like you.

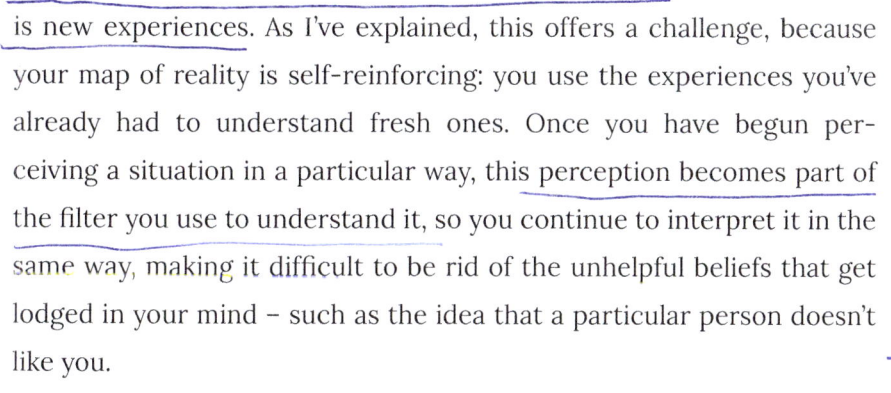

I have an elderly aunt, for example, who has a big problem getting her car in and out of her driveway. To be clear: she's never bumped into anything, has never damaged the car or any cars nearby, and has never been prevented from going out or returning home. But her experience is nonetheless that the driveway is very problematic. Every time she needs to get the car in or out, she expends a huge amount of energy on it. She talks about it, she worries about it, and she simulates a thousand catastrophes in her mind.

In reality, nothing is wrong. In reality, there's no problem at all. But because of the way she looks at the situation, the problem is reconfirmed for her every time she goes in or out of the driveway. My aunt could drive into her driveway a hundred times without any problems, and yet to her mind, her difficulties would still be confirmed every time. Just like me with my boss at the video store until the day he offered me more shifts.

Inquiry

So this is the challenge. The only way to change your beliefs is to have new experiences, but the self-reinforcing nature of your map of reality suppresses these experiences. As such, it is a natural process for your brain to construct beliefs, but there is no corresponding natural process to break them down again.

What do you do?

Inquiry.

You consciously decide to reexamine your experiences to see if they are, in fact, as true as your map of reality would have you believe.

My aunt could drive into the driveway a hundred times, and her difficulties would be confirmed each time. Or, just once, she could explore what is actually going on when she goes in and out but do so with an open mind.

That is the crucial thing.

And that's what Inquiry is all about.

Inquiry is a way of questioning what you believe. An open and curious investigation into the stressful thoughts that are the real cause of your suffering. A way of putting question marks by the experiences you think you've had, allowing you to discover new possibilities besides the ones you are so painfully sure are true. Deliberately creating, one could say, the process I went through when my boss at the video store offered me more shifts, and this new experience changed my map of reality, and as such, shifted my entire perspective.

A Workshop That Went Wrong

Let me share an example. About twenty years ago, having just founded my company, I was given one of my first big jobs. I was in my twenties, keen to prove myself and come across as professional and competent. My client was a large firm, and I met with one of the directors for a briefing, developed a concept for the workshop, and ping-ponged ideas back and forth with him as I sorted out all the details. The workshop, which focused on ways to handle stress and conflict, involved about three hundred participants and went extremely badly. The whole set-up was wrong. The participants were less able to work independently than I had been told, I had far too few assistants, and my workshop came immediately after a lecture that struck a totally different note so none of them were prepared for the headspace I was trying to create. They were some of the most painful hours of my life.

After the event, I met with the director again, and he informed me he would only pay half the sum we had agreed upon because I hadn't delivered what I'd promised. He needed to show the rest of the company that I accepted my share of the responsibility for that fact that the workshop didn't go well.

I thought that was an unreasonable demand. I had worked hard, I had discussed things with him beforehand, and everything I had arranged was based on the information he had provided me. I had done my bit and had put in a lot of work, and I felt he was using me as part of his own internal game at the firm. I didn't want to fight with him over the money, so I agreed to his suggestion, but I left the meeting with a sense of injustice that remained with me for years. Every time I saw the company's logo somewhere, a wave of unpleasantness washed through me, and my fear of ending up in the same situation again was a source of stress every time I took on jobs that reminded me of that one.

Questioning My Beliefs

This feeling stuck around for many years before it suddenly dawned on me one day how much unpleasantness I was inflicting on myself by holding onto this story. Everybody else had long since forgotten all about it, and I was the only one still suffering from my insistence on being in the right. So I decided to explore the issue one more time.

'He treated me unfairly' – was that really true?

When I stopped looking only for those things that confirmed my story and instead submerged myself in my memory of the experience with an open mind, I began to see a whole series of things I had previously been blind to. I could see myself as a young man, eager to seem competent and professional, and I could see how there had been a lot of uncertainties that I was too unsure of myself to probe more deeply. I realized that, ultimately, it was *my* responsibility to obtain the briefing I required. I was the one who knew what information I needed – how was he supposed to know that? On reflection, it crossed my mind that he had, in fact, said he thought it all sounded a bit crazy, but that if I was sure it would work, he would trust me. And because I had been so busy trying to seem convincing and reliable, I had completely dismissed his concerns.

The deeper I looked into the experience, the clearer it became to me that insofar as mistakes had been made, I was the one who had made them. I was the one who hadn't done my job properly, and indeed, I should be grateful he had offered to pay me as much as he did. The situation was the exact opposite of what I had thought. He hadn't treated me unfairly at all – quite the contrary. I was the one who had treated him unfairly by clinging onto my negative story about him all those years. And I had treated myself unfairly, too, by clinging to my painful perception.

It took nearly fifteen years before it occurred to me to question this story, look myself in the eye, and challenge my conviction that I was in the right. The process itself didn't take more than half an hour, and with it came a physical wave of relief, that was like a stone falling from my heart – a stone I had been carrying around for all that time.

You Can't Let Go of Your Beliefs

You can't let go of your beliefs. You can't decide to change your map of reality. It's impossible, just as it's impossible to change your production of saliva simply by making up your mind to do so. But you can *question* your beliefs. You can examine them with an open mind. And as you discover where your map of reality is off, you see through them, and the moment you do so, they lose their hold on you.

It's like being at the airport, having arrived early and taking your time to browse through the shops, when you suddenly realize that you've spent way longer than you thought and that your gate is closing in just a few minutes. A wave of panic almost knocks you out as you grab your luggage and rush through the crowd, frantically searching for the signs that point toward your gate. You check your watch several times as you sprint across the terminal, trying to decide how fast you must run to make it. How could this happen? You had planned everything so well! Then, as you skid around a corner, glancing at your watch one more time, you suddenly realize that you're mistaken. It's only 6.55, not 7.55. You saw the clock hands wrong. You have almost an hour to burn! And of course, the minute you recognize this, you return from your state of heightened alert. It may take a few moments for the biochemical reactions to wash out of your system, but you are no longer panicking.

This is the first thing to notice: the change is immediate. The instant you realize your misunderstanding, there's no more panic.

The second thing to notice is that once you've seen the clock correctly, you can't make yourself see it wrong again. You can't convince yourself back into believing that you're running late. You can't 'unsee' what you've seen, so to speak.

Inquiry Causes Natural Changes in Your Map of Reality

This is what it's like to see through your beliefs. You believe that you're out of time; you are stressed out; you investigate; and you realize: you're not in a hurry at all.

Inquiry is not about actively installing new beliefs or trying to re-program our unconscious mind through affirmations or self-suggestion. It's about seeing for yourself by examining with an open mind. As such, when you're doing Inquiry, you're working *with* the system, not against it. It's an entirely organic process. Your nervous system is designed to construct and constantly readjust a map of reality based on your experiences. So, when your experiences change, your map of reality changes too. And this is what happens when you do Inquiry. You exploit functions that are already naturally inherent in you.

When my boss told me that he considered me a good worker at the video store, the effect was immediate. My perception of the situation changed, making me think about it differently, look at it differently, and experience it differently – so I reacted differently. Just as I would react differently today if I met the director from the firm where I conducted my unsuccessful workshop, because I see the situation in a new light after having investigated it. And this is not something that requires any continued effort on my part. There is nothing I need to 'maintain' or hold on to, I don't need to remind myself that I'm not in a hurry. I have seen it. And what I've seen won't suddenly become unseen.

In that sense, Inquiry is simple – all it requires is an open mind. Especially when you're just getting started, however, opening your mind can feel somewhat unusual. Your mind has a natural preference for stability, and you may have been raised to see shifts in your opinions as signs of weakness. Therefore, it can be helpful to have a structure to support you as you begin your work with Inquiry, and in my experience, no structure is better to start with than *The Work of Byron Katie*.

CHAPTER 5

THE WORK OF BYRON KATIE

Byron Katie is a contemporary American woman who realized one day exactly what I'm claiming here: it's our thoughts that are the cause of our problems, and the various forms of emotional stress or pain we experience are due not to reality but to the way we *think* about reality.

At the time, she knew nothing about psychology or philosophy, about how our nervous systems work or about any of the long traditions of thought that have been devoted to investigating these matters before us. She simply dove in herself, and she gradually developed a practice that in my opinion has turned out to be one of the most impactful and sophisticated ways to work with the challenges of the mind in the context of our modern day and age.

I find *The Work of Byron Katie* (which is also known as *Inquiry Based Stress Reduction* (IBSR) but is most commonly referred to simply as *The Work*) to be one of the best forms of Inquiry available – especially when you're just getting started. Both because it offers a clearly structured process and because of its signature concept of 'turnarounds,' which in my experience is a very powerful support for those who are new to Inquiry.

The Work consists of three parts:

1. Identifying your beliefs,
2. Asking a series of questions known as 'the four questions,' and
3. Working with the turnarounds.

Let me give you a quick overview of each of them.

Identifying Your Beliefs

The first part of any Work session is to identify the beliefs that you're going to work on. In The Work, the invitation is to also try to find a specific situation to work on, where these beliefs are active. In the example of my unsuccessful workshop, my belief is: 'He is treating me unfairly,' and the situation is at the meeting with the director when he says that he is only willing to pay half my fee.

The Work offers several different ways of identifying the beliefs that are causing our difficulties. In some cases, as in the situation with the director, it is very straightforward to pick up what I'm believing, but sometimes, it requires a little more work to find out exactly what it is that is causing our stress. In part, because, very often, our trouble isn't caused by one single belief, but rather by a cluster of different beliefs, supporting and reinforcing each other. (I will return to this matter of how to untangle clusters of different beliefs in Chapter 6).

The Four Questions

Once you have identified a situation and the beliefs you want to work on, the second part of the process is examining these beliefs one at a time using the four questions of The Work.

The four questions are:

1. 'Is it true?'
2. 'Can you absolutely know that it's true?'
3. 'How do you react, what happens when you believe that thought?'
4. 'Who would you be without that thought?'

The purpose of the four questions is to help you re-experience what is actually going on inside you when you believe a thought; what it costs you to believe it; and how believing it affects your behavior. It's like doing a slow-motion replay of the situation, noticing all the details that elude you when you're caught in the fixed perspectives of your story, and then experiencing what life would be like without it.

The Turnarounds

Experiencing the actual price of believing your thoughts (question 3) and the potential benefits of letting go of them (question 4) activates your nervous system and motivates your unconscious to look for better strategies. And so, your mind opens to the third part of the process, the turnarounds.

When working with the turnarounds, your task is to *find examples of how opposite variations of what you believe are as true or truer*. Especially for people who are new to Inquiry, this can be a bit of a challenge. I will walk you through the details later – for now, let me just say that one way of turning statements around is to their direct opposite. In my aunt's case, that would be 'it is *easy* to park the car in the driveway.' And her task would then be to find genuine examples of how this turned-around statement is *as true* or perhaps *even truer* than the original. In the example of the director, the turned-around statement would be 'he is treating me *fairly*.'

This is where our willingness to open our minds is put to the test. The task is not to just come up with clever thoughts. The task is to find *genuine* examples, that is: examples that are true for us. Which is a lot easier if we are thorough as we go through answering the four questions first.

Inquiry is About Experience, Not Analysis

It's very easy to misunderstand The Work and think that it's a purely intellectual process. That answering the four questions is about using a lot of words or that finding examples of the turnarounds is a matter of philosophical speculation or like a lawyer arguing his case before a jury. But that's a misperception. It's not an analysis we're after when we do Inquiry. We're not looking for rational arguments or logical explanations. And we're not trying to trick or convince ourselves about anything either. Inquiry is about *honesty*. It's about facing ourselves and the hidden structures that determine our behavior. And in The Work, you do so by entering your inner simulator and giving yourself time to relive the situation you're working with, finding answers to your questions *in* that experience instead of trying to come up with them by thinking about it.

In that sense, Inquiry is a form of meditation. It takes stillness. It's a process of slowing down and being truly present with yourself. This is the key point: inquiry takes stillness. It's so tempting to try to think our way out, but it doesn't work. It's not a lack of knowledge that makes you eat that extra slice of chocolate cake while you're on a diet, and it's not because you don't know that smoking is unhealthy that you can't quit. Changing your map of reality comes down to experiences in your nervous system, not acquiring new information. It's not enough to know intellectually. You need to be as absorbed as possible in your inner simulations, so you are mentally and emotionally present in the situation you're working with. Because when you're in that state, your whole body is involved, and that's when you begin to form new experiences.

As long as you remember that, The Work is simple. Don't go *hunting* for answers and examples. When you examine how you react when you believe a particular thought, don't arrive at your answers by thinking about them. *Experience* them. Experience what it's like to be in that situation believing that thought. What images show up inside? Which emotions occur? How do you act in the situation? How do you treat those around you? Ask the questions and wait for the examples to show up by themselves. Slow things down and become aware of all the unconscious processes that cause both your emotional state and the perceived limits on what you're able to do. The better you get at observing in yourself these concealed processes, and the better you get at turning them around and *experiencing* that the truth is often the opposite of what you think, the more your beliefs let go of you, and as they do, peace and freedom fill your world.

EXERCISE: **BECOMING STILL**

Most people recognize the difference between having a normal, everyday chat with somebody and having a deep conversation with their best friend. In principle, the subject matter might well be the same, but there are very significant differences between the two conversations.

Doing The Work means engaging in the deep conversation. As I've written several times, it's about becoming still. It's about slowing down and noticing all the little details; about being truly present in your experience. It's that inner state when you're sitting around a campfire, gazing into the embers while the night grows dark around you. It's the sound of the ocean waves and the deep, peaceful breathing of a loved one lying next to you. It's the soft music of a cello, the deep roots of a tree, the dull thud of a galloping horse. It's opening to the deep wisdom within. It's a stone sinking toward the bottom of a quiet lake. It's letting your breathing draw you deeper and deeper into yourself, all the way inside to the place where everything becomes still.

> Try to go there now. Turn your attention to your breath. Relax the palms of your feet. Relax your hands. Relax your forehead. Let your lips become soft. Notice the rhythm of your breath and allow it to deepen. Feel your body from the inside. Let go of any tension in your shoulders, in your back, and in your face. Slow down. Close your eyes and simply breathe for a couple of minutes.
>
> For some, this shift into a state of introspection and experience-based perception is easy and familiar, while for others, it's a more extended process. But everybody can do it. It's simply a matter of slowing down and turning your attention inward.

Example: Firing an employee

Let's look at an example of using the four questions and the turnarounds together.

Imagine you're a manager in a company and you have to inform an underperforming employee that she's being let go. It's a working environment where you know each other well, so you're aware that the employee is undergoing some challenges in her personal life.

She's newly divorced, has two small children, and lives in a house which she can't really afford.

For most managers, this situation would trigger some conflicting thoughts. Maybe you'd be thinking something along the lines of, 'She'll go to pieces if I fire her,' 'It'll be a catastrophe for her,' 'She'll never find another job at the same pay grade,' 'She'll be forced to leave her home.'

If you believe these thoughts, letting her go will be a very unpleasant experience. The process will take up a lot of headspace, and when you give her the news, you'll be uncomfortable and ill at ease. And for obvious reasons – after all, you believe you're about to send a woman packing into her worst nightmare.

Asking the Four Questions

The question is whether what you believe is actually true. Is it true that it would be catastrophic for her to be fired (question 1)? Can you absolutely know that it's true (question 2)?

How do you react when you believe the thought that it would be a catastrophe for her (question 3)? You feel guilty. You feel trapped between your role as a boss and your perception of who you are as a person. One awful scenario after another pops up in your mind. You focus energy on pondering what you could do to ameliorate her problems. You put off the dismissal, creating a sense of frustration among the rest of the staff because they must do extra work to correct her mistakes. As such, you undermine your authority and engender mistrust in your abilities as a manager. When you actually have to deliver the news, you are unclear and flustered, becoming brusque and harsh in your attempts to hide your mixed feelings. Or perhaps you become apologetic, offering excuses and beating around the bush. You don't give her clear feedback about how things got to this point. Afterward, you try to avoid meeting her in the corridor, and when you get home, you ransack the kitchen cabinets for anything sugary and feel uneasy the whole weekend.

Who would you be if you *didn't* believe the thought that being fired would be a catastrophe for her (question 4)? Who would you be, sitting across from her in your office, looking her in the eyes, if you didn't – couldn't – believe that this is going to be a catastrophe for her? Calm. Poised. Kind. Clear. You would be able to listen; consider her response; take your time. The process wouldn't siphon attention away from your other tasks. And you would be able to help organize farewell drinks, giving a good and honest speech in which you lauded her many positive qualities.

Turning the Thought Around

Having investigated your reactions using the four questions, you are ready to move to the turnarounds. Let's again focus on the turnaround to the extreme opposite: 'It would be a *blessing* for the employee to be fired.'

Could that, in fact, be just as true?

As things currently stand, she has a job she's not really qualified for. You know from what she has told you that she feels constantly under pressure. Because of her living situation, she's struggling to stay within her budget. She doesn't have enough time or energy for her children. She feels guilty about her colleagues. And she's only hanging onto the job because she needs the money. Being let go will liberate her from all of that.

Yes, she may have to move, but can you know with any kind of certainty that it won't be the best thing that could happen for her? Can you know with any kind of certainty that a change of scenery isn't exactly what she needs? A new job, new neighbors, new colleagues?

Nobody knows the future. All we know are our thoughts about it, and they are pure guesswork.

The Turnarounds are not an Attempt to Manipulate Reality

Working with the turnarounds is not about trying to convince yourself into some airy-fairy alternate reality where you naively close your eyes to what's real. On the contrary – it's about seeing reality for what it is.

In this example, it's true that it could be a catastrophe for her, and it's good to be sensitive to that. It is, however, equally true that it could be a blessing. How many times have you met people who said that what looked like a disaster at the time turned out to be the best thing that ever happened to them? How many times have you yourself experienced how disruptions in your life were actually opportunities in disguise?

To support your survival, your mind is conditioned to always look for the worst-case scenarios, and that's fine. But when you lock yourself into those fixed positions to a point where they are the only options you can see, it becomes a problem. Working with the turnarounds is a way of opening your mind to more possibilities. The more limiting beliefs you see through, the less friction there is between you and what's going on around you, and the easier it is to act with straightforward, spontaneous and effortless kindness.

If there's an employee who isn't doing a good enough job, and if your mind is open, there is nothing stopping you from noticing it, talking to her about it and, if necessary, letting her go. If your job is to ensure that the department functions properly, and if your mind is clear, then none of your personal stories will get in the way of your ability to carry out that job. Which doesn't mean you'll become cold and uncaring. On the contrary. When you're no longer getting in your own way with all your stories, you become someone who can be depended on; someone who is warm and connected, while at the same time, direct and honest.
In my experience, that is what true kindness looks like.

Who Would You Be Without Your Beliefs?

Who would you be without your beliefs? When my boss came into the video store, who would I have been if I hadn't believed what I believed? 'He doesn't think I'm doing a good enough job.' 'I need to get him to like me.' All my problems were due to my beliefs and my attempts to manipulate the world according to them. Who would I have been if I had been able to distinguish between fiction and reality? A young man putting videos on a shelf. A relaxed, friendly, obliging employee.

Who would you be if you could see the mess in your children's rooms without all your beliefs? Someone deciding whether to tidy up. 'They'll never learn!' Is that true? What would it be like to meet them without this belief?

Who would you be if you could have a discussion with your boyfriend without thinking that his tone is disrespectful? Someone who listens. 'When he raises his voice, it means he doesn't respect me!' Is that true? Could it actually mean that he respects you enough to be honest? And even if it is true, who would you be if you realized that his stories have nothing to do with you?

Who would you rather be fired by? A stressed-out, unapproachable and muddled manager who tries to avoid you? Or a clear, accommodating and warm manager who gives a speech at your farewell drinks?

PART 3

THE WORK
- How to do Self-Inquiry

WAITING FOR SOMEONE ELSE TO CHANGE

IS THE LONG ROAD TO HAPPINESS.

— BYRON KATIE

CHAPTER 6

IDENTIFY YOUR THOUGHTS

It's difficult to explain the effect of this work to someone who hasn't yet experienced it first-hand.

I try to express things in a way that makes sense in my map of reality, and when you translate it through all the filters of your understanding, you end up with something very different. I'm sure many of the things I've said so far have raised questions and maybe even caused concerns. I've been explaining this to thousands of people over the years, and I've been met with many reservations, 'buts' and 'ifs.' My general experience is that those who overcome these reservations, however, and put things to the test, all find the same thing: that what they thought they'd understood wasn't it, and that their concerns were unnecessary.

Inquiry is not what you think it is. It's much more and much better. I know from experience that what I'm sharing here can have a huge effect on your life. And make no mistake: I mean a *huge* effect. There is, however, one absolutely crucial requirement for it to work: *practice*. It isn't something you can learn by reading – it relies on you actually *doing* something.

So that's my invitation.

In what follows, I will tell you everything you need to know to begin experimenting with Inquiry, and I will also point you to the right places for further support. If I could do the work for you, I would be happy to do that as well, but I can't. I can only emphasize how unique an opportunity this is. By some stroke of genius (or fate, or coincidence), you have ended up with this book in your hands, and for whatever reason, you've read half of it. The number of events that had to come together to produce that result is mind-boggling. I know how powerful the process is. And so far, I've not met anyone who sincerely wanted to do Inquiry, who couldn't do it. The ball, in other words, is entirely in your court, and there's a direct path from this moment to the life of joy, peace, and freedom that you long for. Isn't that amazing? And it only hinges on one thing: will you set aside your natural reservations and put my words to the test?

I hope you will.

Getting Started: How to Do The Work

As I explained in the previous chapter, The Work consists of three parts.

- First, you identify the thoughts you have come to believe in a given situation.
- Next, you investigate each thought using 'The Four Questions.'

- Finally, each time you have done so, you take the investigated thought and 'turn it around' to various view-points, contemplating genuine examples of how each turned-around version of the thought might be just as true as the original.

Let's start by understanding how The Work goes about collecting thoughts to work on.

How to Solve the Challenge of Seeing Your Own Map of Reality

One of the challenges we meet when we want to work with our beliefs is that they can be very difficult to see. Just as we can't look directly at our own eyes, we can't 'look' directly at our map of reality.

The Work offers a very elegant solution to this problem.

In the same way as you use a mirror to see your eyes, you can use the world to see your beliefs. As I've tried to explain, the world means nothing in and of itself. It's only when *you* look at it that it acquires meaning, and this meaning is, therefore, a reflection of your beliefs.

As such, by working with what you believe about the world, you are in fact working directly with your map of reality: 'My boyfriend doesn't respect me.' 'My boss is unreasonable.' 'Getting fired will be a catastrophe for her.' 'My children will never learn to tidy up.' All these judgments are doorways to your inner world, and when you do The Work, they are a perfect place to start.

The 'Judge-Your-Neighbor Worksheet'

So when doing The Work, you focus on the judgments you put on the world around you. You focus on everything you think is wrong about other people, your surroundings, and the things that happen to you, because these unquestioned beliefs are the essence of your struggle with reality and, as such, the cause of your problems.

To support you in collecting these thoughts, one of the fundamental tools of The Work is the so-called 'Judge-Your-Neighbor Worksheet.' As the name indicates, this worksheet is a way of gathering together all your judgments about another person, and the best way to fill it in is to focus on a *specific situation*.

As I've explained earlier, the more involved your nervous system is in your Inquiry, the greater the effect. The easiest way of activating your whole nervous system is by imagining something very concrete. Just like when you imagine biting into a lemon.

To understand this, consider the difference between speaking in general terms about the challenges you face when you have teenagers living at home and speaking about the specific conflict you had with your son the day before yesterday when he was lying on the sofa and refused to help lay the table.

When you just speak in general terms, you drift from one vague image to the next, largely thinking in terms of theories and statistics. When you find yourself back in the concrete situation and relive your disappointment and the frustration you felt as he stomped off into his room, something completely different happens. Your emotions reassert themselves, the inner images, the physical feeling of your anger, and the urge to shout, come back. Your inner simulator is then in full flow, and you *experience* what you're working on, speaking *from* a specific situation instead of *about* it. This is when The Work truly begins to take effect.

An Example of a Filled-In Judge-Your-Neighbor Worksheet

Here is an example of a Judge-Your-Neighbor Worksheet that I've completed about the situation with my son on the sofa:

THE SITUATION

My son is lying on the sofa watching TV, and when I ask him to help lay the table, he says, 'Why should I?'. The specific moment I'm working with is just as he's saying that.

1. **In this situation, who angers, confuses, saddens, or disappoints you, and why?**
   I am angry **with** my son **because** he won't do his chores.

2. **In this situation, how do you want them to change? What do you want them to do?**
   I want my son **to** do as I tell him. I want him to take responsibility. I want him to do as he promised. I want him to contribute to the household.

3. **In this situation, what advice would you offer to them?**
   My son **should** remember how much we do for him. He shouldn't opt out. He shouldn't be so sullen.

4. **In order for you to be happy in this situation, what do you need them to think, say, feel, or do?**
   I need my son **to** change his mind. I need him to get up and get started. I need him to be happy to help.

5. **What do you think of them in this situation? Make a list.**
   My son **is** lazy, unreasonable, teenager-y, ridiculous, only sees the short-term.

6. **What is it about this situation that you don't ever want to experience again?**
   I don't ever want to experience my son saying no to doing his chores again.

As you can see, filling in the worksheet isn't an attempt to be polite or kind. It's a way of gathering my honest thoughts in a specific moment, and although in my case, it's definitely true that I love my son, and I'm genuinely sympathetic to the challenges intrinsic to being a teenager, those weren't the thoughts that were going through my mind at that particular moment. Which is why I got angry. I might well see the situation differently ten minutes – or for that matter ten seconds – later, but right there, in *that* moment, those were my thoughts.

And the reason I know that is because I returned to the situation in my inner simulator. I didn't do an intellectual analysis of the situation. I didn't try to guess what I *probably* thought or ponder what I believe people *typically* think in such situations. I took myself back to the situation by getting still, sinking into my memories, and becoming completely present with them in my inner simulator. And I didn't begin to respond to the questions on the worksheet before I was fully there, both mentally and emotionally. In this way, I didn't have to guess or approximate. I simply became still and *experienced* what was going on inside me at that moment.

There is No Statute of Limitations on Painful Experiences

You can do this with a situation that happened five minutes ago. You can do it with a situation that happened forty years ago. Painful experiences don't just disappear. As long as they have an emotional charge for us, they stay in there, surprisingly fresh, and as soon as you slow down and become still, the details begin to pop back up again.

Here is a worksheet about a situation from my childhood. I don't think I could have been much more than four or five years old.

THE SITUATION

I'm walking down the street with my mother when a strange man approaches and greets us. I'm shy, but my mother wants me to greet him nicely. The specific moment I'm working with is just as my mother pulls me off her leg and turns me around to greet him.

1. **In this situation, who angers, confuses, saddens, or disappoints you, and why?**
   I feel pressured by my mother because she wants me to greet the stranger.

2. **In this situation, how do you want them to change? What do you want them to do?**
   I want my mother to look after me. I want her to pick me up. I want her to take me away from the man. I want her to tell me it's ok if I don't greet the man.

3. **In this situation, what advice would you offer to them?**
   My mother should notice how unpleasant I think it is. She should hold me in her arms. She shouldn't force me to do something I don't want to. She shouldn't prioritize good behavior above my personal boundaries.

4. **In order for you to be happy in this situation, what do you need them to think, say, feel, or do?**
   I need my mother to protect me. I need her to respect my boundaries. I need her to help me through the situation. I need her to show me it's ok to say no.

5. **What do you think of them in this situation? Make a list.**
   My mother is unreliable, self-centered, demanding, a bad mother.

6. **What is it about this situation that you don't ever want to experience again?**
   I don't ever want my mother to pressure me into doing something I don't want. I never want to be let down by my mother again.

This situation is nearly forty years old, but when I become still and give myself time to be present in it again, I can see it clearly before my inner eye. I'm back there again, able to feel what it was like to be a little boy clinging to his mother's leg. I can't see what the man looked like; I just have a sense of him being an older man in a hat and a long coat. But the feeling of my mother's grip as she pulls me away and turns me around is absolutely clear, and it is there that my emotional response is strongest when I relive the situation today.

Anchor in a Specific Moment in the Situation If You Can

Some situations are quite simple, like this moment from my childhood. I remember nothing of what happened before or afterward, just that fragment of a memory I still carry with me. But when I did Inquiry on the situation, it became clear to me how this feeling of being pushed outside my comfort zone has recurred again and again throughout my life, and how in my adult life, I have repeatedly overstepped my own boundaries, pressuring myself to do certain things when it would have been kinder to give myself a break. At the same time, I can see my mother's innocence in that situation – she wanted her son to be well brought-up and to show the old man (who I would guess was probably a friend of my grandparents) that she had a nice family. And I can see my own innocence when I force myself out of my comfort zone trying to live up to exactly the same kind of expectations today. Nonetheless, after having worked through the situation, something has definitely changed inside me. I have become more sensitive to my own boundaries, and I don't force myself to do things I find unpleasant to the same extent as before. Other situations are more complex, and a single situation can easily result in several different worksheets, all of which contain whole sets of beliefs with many different reactions. That is another reason why it's a good idea to anchor yourself in a specific moment. In the situation with the teenager on the sofa, for example, imagine that he got upset, kicked the table and stomped out of the room, slamming the door behind him and cracking the paint around the doorframe. Each of these moments could give rise to completely new waves of beliefs and with them, different worksheets (see Figure 2).

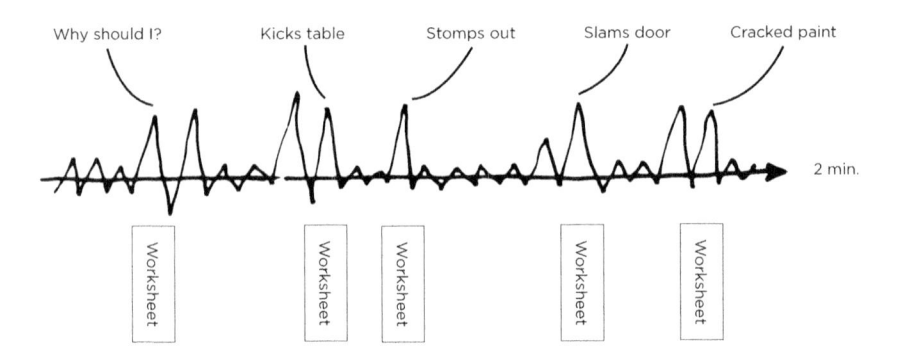

Fig. 2: Several worksheets in the same situation
Our emotional stress level can peak several times during a situation of just a couple of minutes, and each peak can hold its own separate worksheet in the form of its own set of active beliefs.

For this reason, it can be a good idea to not only anchor in a specific situation, but even find a specific moment in that specific situation to write from. Is it the moment when he says, 'Why should I?' Is it when he kicks the table? Or is it when he slams the door?

A worksheet focusing on the moment when I saw the cracked paint around the doorframe would look like this, for instance:

THE SITUATION

My son has just slammed the door to his room, and I see that the paint around the doorframe is cracked. The specific moment I'm working with is right when I notice the cracked paint.

1. **In this situation, who angers, confuses, saddens, or disappoints you, and why?**
   I am angry **with** my son **because** he is destroying our house.

2. **In this situation, how do you want them to change? What do you want them to do?**
   I want my son **to** stop venting his anger on his physical surroundings. I want him to control himself. I want him to behave properly.

3. **In this situation, what advice would you offer to them?**
   My son **shouldn't** get so upset. He should talk about things instead of flipping out. He should count to ten.

4. **In order for you to be happy in this situation, what do you need them to think, say, feel, or do?**
   I need my son **to** close the door carefully, even though he's angry. I need him to get a handle on his temper.

5. **What do you think of them in this situation? Make a list.**
   My son **is** a drama queen, disrespectful, inconsiderate, out of control.

> 6. **What is it about this situation that you don't ever want to experience again?**
> **I don't ever want** my home to be destroyed just because my son can't be bothered to do his chores. I never want to put up with his unreasonable behavior again.

Use Short, Simple Sentences

Focusing on a specific moment in the situation you're working on is a good way to support yourself in making the process of Inquiry easier. And so is filling in the worksheets with short, simple sentences. This is both because it's very easy to get lost in heady mental constructs when our sentences are too complex and because working with the turnarounds is a lot simpler when the sentences you work with are easy to hold in your mind. A helpful trick is to think of how a five-year-old would state things.

Here are a few examples to show you what I mean.

'*I want John to clear things with me when he is in a situation that is politically sensitive and may lead to trouble later on*' is a very long sentence. What makes it long is the specification of the situation in which I want this to happen, and that part can be left out and simply held as context while we work on the core demand: '*I want John to clear things with me.*'

Similarly, '*I want Sarah to ask me first, even if everyone else says that they are sure it will be okay'* becomes unnecessarily long-winded. If you think of how a five-year-old would say this, it could probably be shortened to: *'I want Sarah to ask me first.'*

It's all about making the sentences as simple and clear as possible, without throwing the baby out with the bathwater. Don't cut so deep that you lose the operative elements, but don't try to cram in so many details, either, that your sentence loses its power.

Here is one more example: *'Steve shouldn't think that just because he has more experience than the rest of us, he is the only one who knows how to do it.'* I would probably shorten this one to: *'Steve shouldn't think he's the only one who knows how to do it.'*

In *Appendix A: Worksheet Examples* on page 173, you can see some examples of filled-in worksheets that can give you a sense of the simple sentence structure that lends itself well to the Inquiry process.

Different Situations are Like Different Doors that Lead to The Same Room

It is often those closest to you and those with whom you have the most complex relationships that are the cause of the most challenging reflections of your beliefs. And it is, therefore, from them that you have the most to learn when you begin to do Inquiry. The people you thought were the cause of your biggest problems turn out to be your best teachers. Your children, your partner, your parents, your colleagues, your employees, your boss. They turn out to be central to helping you on your way.

If you have limiting beliefs around a certain topic – such as being treated unfairly, for example – you will project those beliefs onto many people and situations in your life. The situations look new every time, but in reality, it's the same beliefs that are causing all the trouble, be it with your partner, your siblings, at work, or on the soccer field.

Say for example that you have an issue around respect. Let's make it simple and say that when you were growing up, some of your classmates used to take your things and hide your schoolbag. This has made you extremely sensitive to how others treat you, and the result is that you experience yourself being treated disrespectfully in many situations. The way your colleague speaks to you in the meeting feels disrespectful. The way the woman in the supermarket ignores you feels disrespectful. You even experience the way the kids on the street take so long to get out of the way when you return home in the car as disrespectful.

In reality, of course, their behavior has nothing to do with respect. There are a hundred reasons why they act the way they do, and most of them have nothing to do with you. When seen through the lens of *your* particular map of reality, however, lack of respect becomes the meaning you ascribe to them, and consequently, you keep running into people who don't seem to respect you.

Then you do The Work. You pick one – just one – of these situations where you feel disrespected by someone, fill in a Judge-Your-Neighbor

Worksheet and do a deep Inquiry into what's really going on. To your surprise, you realize that the situation has nothing to do with respect. You track the patterns back in time and see how it is your own mind that has been superimposing a story onto reality. You realize that, ultimately, respect is not something you can get from others, and that you can never really know if someone respects you. All you can know is whether you respect you, and when you do, the behavior of others becomes irrelevant. You don't need their respect—you need to respect yourself, and part of that is treating them with respect no matter how they show up. That is how you stay within your own integrity and live in a way that feels true for you.

You've only worked on a single situation out of all the many situations where you felt disrespected, but that's all it takes for all the situations to change. Because all the situations were rooted in the same set of beliefs (see Figure 3), and when that lets go, it shifts your experience across the board, backward in (apparent) time as well as forward. As your map of reality changes, your world changes, and from that moment on, you no longer run into people who disrespect you. Where before, you would have seen people who were disrespectful, now you see people who are confused, who are stressed out, who are thinking about other things, who disagree or who don't understand. Because it never was the world that was the problem. It was believing an interpretation of the world that had been filtered through your unseen and unquestioned beliefs.

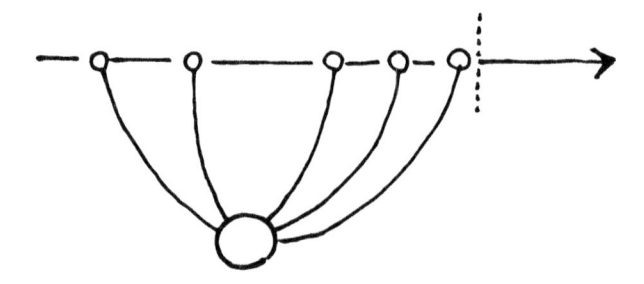

Fig. 3: The same belief shows up in many situations in our life
When you have a set of beliefs around a certain topic (the circle in figure 3), you will project those beliefs onto many situations in your life (the little circles on the timeline), and the same issue will show up in many areas. But when you pick just one of those situations and do Inquiry on it, you see through the beliefs, and as they let go, your view on all those past situations changes, and from this point on (the dotted line on the timeline), as if by magic, those situations no longer show up in your life.

Begin with Whatever is Stressful for You

Every situation that gives rise to emotional stress or unpleasantness involves beliefs you can profitably work with. The sense of unpleasantness wouldn't be there – and in many cases, the memory of the situation wouldn't even be there – if there wasn't something your mind was still struggling with.

It doesn't matter whether it's something that happened five minutes ago or forty years ago. The beliefs that were present in the situation on the street with my mother have stayed with me and affected my behavior throughout my whole life, and I could have found many other such situations that would have given me the opportunity to work through the same issue. They are all doors that lead to the same room; they are part of a single network of roots, all beginning at and so leading to the same point, and when we see the beliefs that have created them for what they are, they all come loose, across both time and space.

One question I often get is, therefore, 'Where should I begin?'; 'Which situation should I work on first?' The answer is simple: begin with any situation that causes you emotional stress or discomfort. It doesn't matter which door you go through. If a situation is emotionally stressful, you can know that there's something worth looking at. The discomfort is the sign; it's like a little voice, whispering in your ear: 'Something's off here.'

Let that voice be your guide.

You Are Reaching a Crucial Point

In a moment, it will be your turn. It's time for you to fill out your first Judge-Your-Neighbor Worksheet. You can either use the one on page 196 or print one out by visiting the resources webpage referenced in *Appendix C: Resources* on page 192.

With this, you reach a crucial point.

Are you ready to take the next, pivotal step and give yourself the gift of experiencing The Work in practice? Are you going to *do* something or are you just going to talk about it? This is it – a defining moment. Take out that worksheet or – if that's too cumbersome – simply find a pencil and a piece of paper and begin to write.

I'm completely sincere when I tell you it could be one of the most important decisions you will ever make. Not because your entire life will immediately change in a sudden flash of insight, but because this simple action is the first step in a process that will transform your life in ways you can't even imagine.

Also, if you *don't* fill out a worksheet now, you will get a lot less from reading the rest of the book. There is a process in play here, and if you skip this step, you will miss many of the finer nuances in what follows.

So. Take yourself seriously. Do it. Whenever you see the start-sign, go to work.

Don't Write Your Worksheet About Yourself

In order to fill out the worksheet, in a minute I will ask you to find a person and a situation to write about. At this point, you might be tempted to write the worksheet about yourself. After all, it's about you, isn't it? So why not go straight to the root of the problem?

The thought makes sense, but in reality, working directly on yourself makes the process less effective. The turnarounds lose their power, and it's far too easy to delude yourself. Remember: what you believe about other people is simply a reflection of what you believe about yourself. It may not be entirely clear to you right now, but as you begin to do this work, it will become obvious. If you want to see yourself clearly, look at your judgments of others. They're all about you.

So yes, you might blame yourself after arguing with someone, and it might feel as if it's your attack on yourself that's the problem. But I invite you to follow the simple directions. Instead of focusing on the moment when you're beating yourself up afterward, go to the moment during the argument when you were, in fact, blaming them, and fill out the worksheet from there.

It's Time to Find a Moment to Write About

In order to find a situation to work with, I invite you to close your eyes and dive into the depths of your mind. You can either look for a stressful situation directly, or you can start with a person who bothers you and then find a situation involving him or her. When did someone make you angry, confused, sad or disappointed? It could be something that happened five minutes ago, or it could be a situation from your distant past – it makes no difference, because whatever happened, if you still feel stressed about it, then the beliefs are still alive in you.

When you have found a specific stressful situation, it's time to return yourself to it one more time. It's time to enter your mind's simulator, travel back to that exact moment and relive it. Where are you? Who are you with? Are you standing or sitting down? What time of day is it?

Bring yourself back fully to the situation, be present in it again, experiencing everything that happened as if it were all happening right now, and when you feel you're there, find the specific moment where the emotion was at its most intense. At what point did your feelings of stress or discomfort peak? What was it the other person said or did – or didn't say or do – that sent that wave of unpleasantness rolling through you?

> Go inside and find a specific moment in a specific situation you want to work on now.

Fill Out Your Worksheet

When you have found that moment and are fully present in it, you are ready to fill out the worksheet. At this point, two things are important:

- Keep returning to the specific moment you've found and allow everything you write to come from your experience at that moment.
- Write in sentences that are as short and simple as possible.

Now all that's left is to get started! Write honestly and without filtering anything. Let yourself be like an unreasonable five-year-old. Don't be considerate. Don't be kind or try to embellish your thoughts. Nobody else is going to read this, so give yourself permission to express yourself with complete freedom.

The more honestly and directly you write down your thoughts, the better the starting point you give yourself to work with later. And if you need any examples of how other people filled out their worksheets, you can find some in *Appendix A: Worksheet Examples* on page 173. Write only one statement for point 1 and write as many statements as you like for the rest of the points, remembering to keep them short and simple.

START Go to work filling out the worksheet now. You can find it in *Appendix C: Resources* on page 192 or you can use the simplified version below.

Think of a recurring stressful situation, a situation that is reliably stressful even though it may have happened only once and recurs only in your mind. As you answer each of the questions below, allow yourself to mentally revisit the time and place of the stressful occurrence. Use short, simple sentences.

1. **In this situation, who angers, confuses, saddens, or disappoints you, and why?**

    I am   [emotion]   with   [name]   because

2. **In this situation, how do you want them to change? What do you want them to do?**

    I want   [name]   to

3. **In this situation, what advice would you offer to them?**

    [name]   should/shouldn't

4. **In order for you to be happy in this situation, what do you need them to think, say, feel, or do?**

   I need [name] **to** _____

   _____

   _____

5. **What do you think of them in this situation? Make a list.**

   [name] **is** _____

   _____

   _____

6. **What is it about this situation that you don't ever want to experience again?**

   I don't ever want _____

   _____

   _____

CHAPTER 7

IDENTIFY YOUR ONELINERS

How did it feel to fill out your first Judge-Your-Neighbor Worksheet? People's reactions differ. Some find it easy, while others find it difficult. Most are surprised by how powerfully their emotional response washes back over them when they write, but that's perfectly natural because our bodies and our emotions react to what's going on in our simulator. So it's a good sign if your emotions were reawakened because it means that you were genuinely present in the situation. Some people like getting all the thoughts that were disturbing them about the situation down on paper. Others find it unpleasant to discover what those thoughts really were.

I will comment further on the worksheets later; for now, it's enough to know that there's no wrong way to fill it out, and that the best way to make them more effective is through working with the content. So let's begin.

Turning Your Oneliners Into Complete Sentences

The worksheet is a means of gathering together your beliefs in a specific moment into a simple form, leaving you with a series of so-called *oneliners* which you can then question one by one.

Under point 2 on the worksheet ('I want [name] to ...'), for example, you could imagine having written the following:

> 2. **I want** Peter **to** listen to me. To ask me when he's not sure about something. To take responsibility for understanding the task. And to judge whether the timeframe is realistic.

Here are four oneliners:

- I want Peter to listen to me.
- I want Peter to ask when he's not sure about something.
- I want Peter to take responsibility for understanding the task.
- I want Peter to judge whether the timeframe is realistic.

Notice how, even if they're not necessarily written like this, every single sentence under point 2 on the worksheet begins with 'I want Peter to ...' The oneliner isn't 'To ask when he's not sure about something.' It's '*I want him* to ask when he's not sure about something.' And the same is true for the other points: 'Peter should / shouldn't ...' is the start of all the oneliners under point 3; 'I need Peter to ...' is the start of all the oneliners under point 4; 'Peter is ...' is the start of all the oneliners under point 5; and 'I don't ever want ...' is the start of all the oneliners under point 6.

So even though the list under point 5 looks like this:

> **5.** Peter **is** frivolous, irresponsible, irritating, superficial and demanding.

… it's actually a series of separate oneliners:

- Peter is frivolous.
- Peter is irresponsible.
- Peter is irritating.
- Peter is superficial.
- Peter is demanding.

The goal in formulating the oneliners is to create short, simple sentences with a clear structure. As you get more experienced, this will probably begin to happen by itself while you fill in the worksheet, but in the beginning, it may take a little tweaking afterward to simplify the sentences you have written.

Focusing the Oneliner in Point 1 and Separating Combined Oneliners

Part of filling out point 1 on the worksheet is to identify the basic emotional state you're in, in the situation. And although you can question anything—even an emotional state—we'll start by only focusing on the part that comes after because in point 1.

In this way:

> 1. **I am** angry **with** Peter **because** he doesn't focus on his tasks.

... can be simplified into:

- Peter doesn't focus on his tasks.

Similarly, you can turn

> 1. **I am** hurt **by** Louise **because** she is mean to me.

... into:

- Louise is mean to me.

These are short, simple sentences that express the basic belief as clearly as possible. Take out your worksheet now and cross out the part of point 1 up to and including 'because.'

As you gain more experience, the sentences you write on the worksheet will become increasingly simple. And you will soon be able to spot that a sentence like this one:

> 2. **I want** Peter **to** listen to me and ask when he's not sure of something.

... actually consists of two oneliners:

- I want Peter to listen to me.
- I want Peter to ask when he's not sure of something.

What You Need to Remember When Working with the Worksheet

So what you need to remember when you're working on a Judge-Your-Neighbor Worksheet is the following:

- Find a concrete situation – ideally a specific moment in that situation – to work on.
- Use your inner simulator to be mentally and emotionally present in the situation when you fill out the worksheet.
- Use short, simple sentences.
- Be honest. Let yourself write directly from your experience, without censoring yourself.
- When you begin to work with the oneliners, only use the bit after 'because' in point 1. (I suggest you simply cross out the part that says 'I am [emotion] with [person] because' on the worksheet you just filled out right away.)
- When you work on the statements under points 2–6, remember to include the start of the oneliner each time: 'I want ...,' 'He should ...,' 'I need ...,' 'He is ...,' 'I don't ever want ...'
- Sometimes a single sentence can contain several oneliners – generally it's when the word 'and' is part of the sentence. 'Caroline should take her time and concentrate' is two oneliners.

Once you've had a bit more practice working with the four questions and the turnarounds, these guidelines will start to seem obvious. But don't turn them into a bunch of rules that must be followed to the letter. As with everything else about The Work, remember that the process is a flow, and that you can't do it wrong. Quite the opposite – the more you experiment, the clearer it will be what works for you and what doesn't. It's all about gaining experience, which hones your understanding so that you find it even easier to do next time around.

The number of oneliners people write on the worksheets varies. Sometimes there are only a couple of them for each point. Other times there are quite a lot. The important thing is to remain present in the situation and write down all the thoughts that cross your mind. Just like working with the questions and the turnarounds, filling out the worksheet is a meditation. The best way to help yourself is to become still, let yourself be immersed in what you're doing, and open your mind to whatever appears.

I have recorded a guided meditation for download to support you in filling out the worksheet. You can find a link for it in *Appendix C: Resources* on page 192.

CHAPTER 8

THE FOUR QUESTIONS

With the worksheet in place, you are now ready for the next stage of the process: using the four questions to begin your Inquiry.

Just as when you filled out the worksheet, the crucial thing here is to be present in the situation in your inner simulator. Take the time to bring yourself back to the moment you want to work on. Where are you? What do your surroundings look like? Who are you with? What sounds do you hear? Do you smell anything? Bring yourself completely back to the experience, only beginning to answer the questions when you're there once more.

There are four questions, and they go like this:

1. Is it true?
2. Can you absolutely know that it's true?
3. How do you react, what happens, when you believe that thought?
4. Who would you be without the thought?

And you will find all these answers *in* the situation. This isn't something you can think or analyze your way to. It isn't something you guess or assume. It's something you *experience*. It's something you observe in yourself by taking things slowly and reliving the moment, investigating all the little corners of your reaction that you didn't notice the first time around because it all went so quickly.

Back to the Video Store: A Demonstration of the Four Questions in Action

Let me demonstrate what answering the four questions can look like. I will use a situation from my time working at the video store, and you can imagine that I've filled out a worksheet where the first oneliner is: 'My boss doesn't think I'm doing my job well enough.'

Here is the concrete situation: I'm standing behind the counter, sorting videos, when my boss walks by. I look up and see an expression on his face that I interpret as disapproval. The specific moment I'm anchored in is just as I see his expression.

Oneliner: 'He doesn't think I'm doing my job well enough.'

1. **Is it true?**
   Yes.

2. **Can you absolutely know that it's true?**
   Yes. [That's how I experience it. Intellectually, I'm aware that I can't actually *know*, of course, since I have no access to his thoughts. But I do feel completely certain that this is how things stand, so the answer that comes to me is a 'yes.']

3. **How do you react, what happens, when you believe the thought that he doesn't think you're doing your job well enough?**

   [Note: in *that* particular moment – just as I see his expression.]

   My stomach clenches. My whole body tenses, and a hot wave of discomfort rushes through me. My pulse quickens. My face burns. I feel guilty. I instantly begin racking my brains for what I did wrong. I think I shouldn't have all the videos lying in a mess on the counter. I see images of his disapproving expression. I see a short film of him sitting in a meeting and discussing my inadequacy with the store manager. I see the manager calling me into a meeting to fire me. I see images of the other employees talking behind my back. I see the manager complaining about me to the ones she's close to. I cringe even more. I feel inept and small. I see images from my past when I had the same feelings: situations from school, situations from Boy Scouts, situations from swimming. I try to get away from the feeling. I attack my boss in my mind. I accuse him of being a bad boss. I shift into victim mode: this is so hard for me. Nobody considers my feelings. Everybody's always out to get me. Nobody thinks I'm good enough. I feel sorry for myself. Again, I see images from previous situations where I felt like this. I find confirmation in those past experiences that I'm completely alone, and that it's hard. My mood shifts to miserable. My body feels heavy. Colors pale around me. The time until my shift ends seems infinitely long. I'd rather be anywhere else. I get irritated by my job. I get irritated at the videos in front of me. I get irritated at my boss. I get irritated at the store-manager. I get irritated at the employees gossiping about me. I think they're all horrible. I get angry and introverted and feel ill at ease. Everything is gray and dark. I don't feel well.

4. **Who would you be without the thought that your boss thinks you're not doing your job well enough?**

[Still just in that moment!]

[It takes some time to move away from the strong feeling of grievance I'm experiencing after having investigated the answers to question 3. But gradually, it fades, and I see myself standing by the counter as the boss walks by, and I see his expression, but this time, I'm completely incapable of believing the thought that he doesn't think I'm doing my job well enough.]

I'm calm. Unperturbed. I'm sorting videos. I breathe. I'm completely unaffected by the fact that my boss is walking past. I'm happy. I've got a good system with a few piles of videos on the counter, and I'm enjoying the process of moving the films around. Physically, I'm relaxed. Where previously, I was completely into my boss's business, more aware of what was happening in him than in myself, now I'm at home in my own skin, and it feels solid, safe, comfortable. I'm at rest in myself. I feel strong. If my boss has any feedback for me, I'm confident that he will tell me. I feel respect for my boss, and at the same time, respect for myself. I like my job. I smile. I feel open and full of confidence.

It's by Genuinely Experiencing Your Answers that They Have an Effect

The Inquiry using the four questions is a shift into slow motion, providing an opportunity both to register some of what you're exposing yourself to when you believe the thought you're working with (question 3) and to experience what it would be like to be present in the situation again *without* believing the thought (question 4).

From a purely neurological perspective, what's happening is that your nervous system is given time to experience how stressful and unpleasant it is to believe the thought, and what the situation would be like without it. And that's an important step to have taken before you continue onto the third stage of the process, where you work with the turnarounds, because it's when your unconscious mind discovers how much pain you're inflicting on yourself when you hold onto the thought – and how much better off you would be without it – that you develop the openness necessary to find examples for the turnarounds that you genuinely think are true.

That's why it's so important that you don't simply *think* about the stress and suffering you put yourself through, but genuinely *experience* it – because it's through this concrete experience that your nervous system discovers that the strategies you used in that moment aren't as optimal as you thought they were. It might well be that it was the best you could do when you were five years old and found yourself in the situation for the first time. But now you're older and wiser, it's time to give your survival strategies a maintenance check and explore other options.

Your turn

But let's not get ahead of ourselves. In a minute, it will be your turn to try answering the four questions.

Choose one of the oneliners on your worksheet. When you're working with an entire worksheet, I would usually suggest that you simply begin at the top and work all the way through, but for this exercise, you can simply pick one that is a real cause of stress for you – one where you feel yourself react inside each time you read it. Phrase it as a short and simple sentence, remembering to only use the part after *because* if it's from point 1, or to include the first part of the sentence if it's from points 2, 3, 4 or 5. If it's from point 6, find another one. We work on the oneliners from point 6 in a slightly different way, so it's best not to tackle those yet.

Then return to the situation in your mind and hold yourself in the specific moment you're working with as you experience your answers to the four questions. Many people find it helpful to write down their answers as keywords along the way – not because they need them for anything afterward, but simply as a way of structuring the process. It's so easy for the mind to drift, and writing your answers down can help you keep your focus. Just don't forget that this is a *meditation*. Give yourself enough time to really be absorbed into the experience. Close your eyes and take the time to let the answers come alive in you. It is this internal experience that is the important thing, not your notes.

A Few Details Before You Begin

One thing it's good to bear in mind when you answer question 3 ('How do you react, what happens, when you believe that thought?') is that it's about *your* reactions. It's not about what the *other* person does or about *why* you react as you do. It's not 'I get angry because I don't think he should act that way. After all, I'm the one who made dinner, and he should be able to understand that when you're part of a group, everybody has to help out. Where would we be if everybody just did what he did and completely ignored their responsibilities?' This isn't a description of how you react. It's an argument for why it's reasonable that you react as you do, and therefore, just a confirmation that what you believe is correct. The word you need to look out for here is *because*. When you say 'because' in answering the four questions, it usually leads to a defense or an argument. You don't need 'because' in your answers. You need to notice your reactions. 'I get angry. I attack him. I defend my point of view.' That is a description of your reaction.

It's worth pointing out here that even 'I get angry' is actually an interpretation. If you observe yourself yet more closely, you will discover that what you call 'getting angry' is, in fact, a series of physical responses: 'My hands tense up, my breath quickens, I feel my cheeks burn, my heart starts to pound, I want to grab him, I want to shout.' You've now moved away from abstract generalizations ('anger') and closer to concrete physical and mental reactions.

The way I visualize it, words like 'anger' (or 'sorrow,' 'annoyance,' 'fear,' etc.) are at the top of a pyramid that consists further down of various concrete physical and mental reactions (see Figure 4). The further you go toward the bottom of the pyramid, the more fleshed-out your observations become, and the more concrete and specific are the reactions you're talking about. In day-to-day life, it's practical to be able to refer to the whole pyramid with a single word like 'anger,' for example, but when you do The Work, it's good to experience more of the pyramid than just this generalized interpretation. It's fine to note that you become what you call 'angry,' but it's also good to register some of the concrete (and often exhausting) inner and outer activities of which this concept is just the tip.

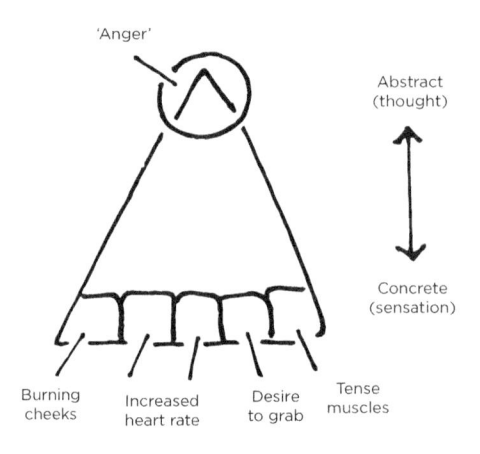

Fig. 4: From abstract concepts to concrete sensations
A term like 'anger' is a mental concept that points to a series of physical and emotional reactions. It is convenient to be able to sum up this combination of inner experiences in a single word, but when you do inquiry, you can support yourself by breaking down these concepts and become aware of all the concrete elements they actually consist of.

Only Answer Yes or No to Questions 1 and 2

Another thing that's helpful to remember is that your answers to questions 1 and 2 ('Is it true?' and 'Can you absolutely know that it's true?') are always either *yes* or *no*. Not 'No, because …' or 'Yes, but …' Just a single syllable. *Yes* or *no*. No arguments. No reasoning. No explanations.

Sometimes it can be difficult to find the answer, but then you just have to wait. I once had a client who took more than half an hour over question 1. She didn't say anything, but there was plenty going on while she considered her answer. And that's just how it is. We can't make the process go any faster. We are witnesses. We pose the questions, then we experience what happens. It's not *seek and find* – it's *ask and wait*. And for questions 1 and 2 the answer can only be *yes* or *no*.

One further thing to note: if the answer to question 1 ('Is it true?') is *no*, then skip over question 2 ('Can you absolutely know that it's true?'). There's no reason to ask this if you have already answered no to question 1. That doesn't mean no is the 'right' answer to the first question – there is no right or wrong answer. Regardless of whether you answered yes or no to the first two questions, you simply experience your responses, then continue on to questions 3 and 4.

Time to Begin

Here are the four questions again:

1. Is it true? [yes/no] (If 'no', skip to question 3)
2. Can you absolutely know that it's true? [yes/no]
3. How do you react, what happens, when you believe that thought?
4. Who would you be without the thought?

Now find a pen and a piece of paper and dive in!

So Much is Happening in a Single Moment

How did it feel to answer the four questions? Were you really present in the situation? Did you take things slowly and experience your reactions? And did you manage to be present again in the situation without the thought?

It's astonishing how much can happen inside us in just a split second. I like to use the image of a complex network of wires, or of the electric cable that crosses the Atlantic, connecting Europe and the USA. It's 2,500 miles long, and yet the moment a connection is made at the other end, electricity instantly runs through the whole thing. It doesn't need time to warm up, and the current doesn't move gradually from one end to the other. The whole thing is instantly alive the moment a connection is made.

It's the same with your complexes of beliefs: the moment somebody presses one of your buttons, the whole network is alive and buzzing with the current. Your exploration when you answer the questions can take some time because you're gradually moving from point to point. But in practice, it's all activated in an instant: the emotional responses, your memories of the past, the fear of where the situation will lead, your reactions to the other person, your view of yourself – it's all triggered at the same time, but it's only when you slow things down and take the time to investigate what's really going on that you realize how many different moving parts there actually are.

CHAPTER 9

THE TURNAROUNDS

You have now investigated your oneliner with the four questions, and you are ready to continue on to the turnarounds.

The turnarounds are where The Work really begins to take effect. If the four questions are a kind of massage for your mind, then the turnarounds are chiropractic. Here you ask your mind to find evidence for the exact opposite of what it believes. As discussed above, this requires an open mind, but it's precisely this process of opening that is your way home.

When you experience that you have a problem, it's always because you've got stuck in a particular, limiting way of viewing the world. You've got caught up in a belief that means you can't see your situation from a wider perspective – you've got blinkers on, so to speak. But the more narrow and inflexible you are in terms of your perspective on what's happening, the more resistance you will experience from the world. And the more open and curious you can be, the more you will experience what's happening as a blessing and an inspiration – and the more you will be able to see the possibilities inherent in the situation, working *with* it instead of against it.

The question is whether you are willing to give up the illusion that you know the truth.

The Difference Between an Objective Truth and an Individual Perspective

I remember a course I gave once where one of the participants turned up a while after we had already started. He came in, took off his coat, sat down on the chair without a word and began to participate in the conversation as if nothing had happened. I was amused by the way he handled the situation, so I asked about it, and it turned out that he had no idea he was late. He thought the course didn't start until nine, and that we were just chatting.

What's interesting is that the rest of us had arrived on time, being ready to start at eight. But he had *also* arrived on time. He'd got up, had breakfast and driven to where the course was taking place, exactly as he'd planned. He was just working on a different basis: he thought that 'on time' meant nine o'clock.

In a world where there are objective truths, you could obviously say that he was late. But if we look at the situation from an individual perspective (the only perspective that really exists), then he arrived on time. Just as the couple who split up actually respected each other and the director from the workshop that went wrong didn't treat me unfairly.

The Opposite of a Profound Truth May Well Be Another Profound Truth

Working with the turnarounds is a way to realize exactly that. They are a particular way of turning your oneliners around, finding examples of how the turned-around oneliners are just as true as the original ones. The statement 'He was late' can, for instance, be turned around to 'He wasn't late.' And your task is then to find concrete examples of how this turned-around statement is also true (in your experience) in the situation.

In the example above, for instance, it's true for me that he wasn't late because:

1. He arrived when he thought he was supposed to.

2. He ended up learning what he was supposed to.
(He wasn't too late to benefit from the course.)

3. In the situation, it was actually a good thing that he arrived when he did, because it gave me a perfect opportunity to demonstrate how more than one truth can co-exist. (In other words, he arrived at exactly the right moment.)

As the famous physicist and Nobel Prize-winner Niels Bohr put it, 'The opposite of a profound truth may well be another profound truth.' That's precisely what the turnarounds can show you. When you let go of your fixed notions of right and wrong and open yourself up to real reality, where things are never unambiguous, you can find the positive and the negative in everything.

The Three Types of Turnaround

The Work works with three kinds of turnaround:

- The turnaround to the opposite.
- The turnaround to the self.
- The turnaround to the other.

There is no fixed order in which you're supposed to work the turnarounds. The order I'm presenting them in here is because that allows for a simple build-up of my explanations. You can start anywhere you like, and if you find one of them to be particularly challenging, it can even be helpful to leave it for a bit, do the others, and then return to it again and see if it's become easier. My general advice with this – as with everything around The Work – is: don't overcomplicate things. For simplicity, I am presenting this as a set of rules, but please don't take them too seriously. On the one hand, sticking to the structure may support you in noticing valuable turnarounds, even when they seem odd at first. On the other hand, don't get so caught up in the mathematics of it that you lose touch with your depth and silence. Don't forget: this is a meditation, not a crossword puzzle. And with that word of caution, let's dive in.

The Turnaround to the Opposite

The turnaround to the opposite can be found in two ways:

- You can add or remove the word 'not;'
- Or you can insert the word you experience as the opposite in the situation.

For example:

> **He is sad**
>
> He is *not* sad [adding the word 'not']
>
> He is *happy* [inserting a word that is the opposite of sad]

Often, there is so little difference between the two versions that you only need to work with one of them. It can even be difficult sometimes to find a word that means the opposite. What is, for example, the opposite of 'read?'

> **I want him to read the book**
>
> I *do not* want him to read the book
>
> I want him to *unread* the book (?)

In other cases, there can be several variations for a single turnaround. Often, 'not' can be inserted in several places, for example:

> **I want him to apologize**
>
> I *do not* want him to apologize
>
> I want him to *not* apologize

Which variations work depend on the context and the person questioning the thought. For most people, it will probably not make a lot of sense to work with 'I want him to unread the book,' but sometimes it does. If it opens something up for you, go for it. And if not, simply move on to the next variation.

Here are a few more examples:

> **He should behave properly**
> He *shouldn't* behave properly
> He should behave *badly*

> **He should think it through**
> He should *not* think it through
> He should be *rash*

In the examples above, for me, the opposite of 'proper' is 'bad' and the opposite of 'thinking it through' is 'being rash.' For you, other opposite words may feel more appropriate, and then you should use those, of course. It's your map of reality, your turnarounds, your Work.

The Turnaround to the Self

The next turnaround is the turnaround to the self. It's very simple:

- Insert yourself into the oneliner in place of everyone else.

For example:

> **He is annoyed**
> *I* am annoyed

> **He doesn't respect me**
> *I* don't respect *myself*

> **I want him to apologize to Mary**
> I want *me* to apologize to *myself*

> **He should behave properly toward Peter**
> *I* should behave properly toward *myself*

The Turnaround to the Other

The last turnaround is the turnaround to the other. The idea is to shift people around in the oneliner to experience how everything you think others are doing to you, you are in fact doing to them.

- Swap the pronouns

> **He is hurting me**
> *I* am hurting *him*

For example:

> **He disrespects me**
> *I* disrespect *him*

> **He is annoyed with me**
> *I* am annoyed with *him*

> **He shouldn't treat me that way**
> *I* shouldn't treat *him* that way

> **I want him to see me clearly**
> I want *me* to see *him* clearly

This turnaround isn't always possible since it requires more than one person to be mentioned in the oneliner. 'He is a fool,' for example, does not allow us to shift anyone around, because there is no one to swap 'him' with. You can do 'I am a fool,' but that's not a turnaround to the other, because there is no swapping of anyone. That is the turnaround to the self.

In other cases, there are several people mentioned in the oneliner, and in those cases, do a turnaround directed at each of them:

> **I want Peter to apologize to Ann**
> I want *me* to apologize to *Ann*
> I want *me* to apologize to *Peter*

In theory, you can also do:

> I want *Ann* to apologize to *Peter*

> I want *Peter* to apologize to *me*

But both of these versions are in other people's business – they are new things you want other people to do – and so, in most cases, they will lead away from yourself and into new stories. And sometimes there may be value in that, so: no fixed rules! (But watch out. It's very easy to get lost. When in doubt, keep it simple.)

The Turnarounds

Here is an overview of the three types of turnarounds:

1. The turnaround to the other
   - Swap the pronouns

2. The turnaround to the self
   - Insert yourself in place of everyone else in the oneliner

3. The turnaround to the opposite
   - Add or remove the word 'not'
   - Insert the word you experience as the opposite in the situation

The turnaround for no. 6

You turn around all the oneliners on the Judge-Your-Neighbor Worksheet like this. There is only one exception, and that is the turnaround for point 6 ('I don't ever want to experience …'), which is the last point on the worksheet.

Point 6 is turned around as follows:

> **I don't ever want to experience Peter not respecting me again**
> *I am willing* to experience Peter not respecting me again
> *I look forward* to experiencing Peter not respecting me again

This is a way of testing the waters in terms of where you are with the situation you're working on. If you can say 'I'm willing to …' and 'I look forward to …' and genuinely mean it, then your work is done. This goes for situations where you will be meeting Peter at work tomorrow, and for situations where Peter has been dead for years, and the only place you meet him is in your mind. One way or the other, this is what The Work holds in store for you: to find a place within yourself where you are willing to experience – and look forward to experiencing – anything life can throw at you. The closer you get to that, the less there is to be afraid of, and the more free and peaceful your life will become.

The Important Part of Working with Turnarounds is Finding Examples

So far, I've been presenting the turnarounds as if they're mainly a semantic exercise. But they're not, of course. The semantics are the smallest part of working with the turnarounds. The main part is finding the examples.

When we've taken a oneliner through the four questions and identified one of its turnarounds, our task is *to find examples of how the turned-around oneliner is as true as – and sometimes even more true than – the original oneliner.*

Let me repeat that. Working with the turnarounds consists of two parts:

1. Find a turnaround
2. Find examples of how this turnaround is as true as or perhaps even truer than the original oneliner

In the story about the director who would only pay half my fee after the unsuccessful workshop, for instance, I believed that he treated me unfairly. I did The Work, answering the four questions, and when I reached the turnarounds, I discovered that it was actually I who had treated *him* unfairly by thinking badly of him in a situation where, in fact, he had met me halfway. I also discovered that I had treated *myself* unfairly by clinging to a story that created so much pain in myself. The truth is that he had treated me extraordinarily *fairly*. He was in the right. And he had still offered to pay me half of the fee for my work.

I will put that in a more structured format for clarity:

Situation: At meeting after the workshop
Moment: Just as he says he will only pay half of my fee
Oneliner: 'He treats me unfairly'

Turnaround: I **treat** *him* **unfairly**

Example:	I thought badly of him in a situation where he met me halfway

Turnaround: I **treat** *myself* **unfairly**

Example:	I caused myself pain by clinging to an untrue story for years

Turnaround: **He treats me** *fairly*

Example:	He was in the right, and he still offered to pay half my fee

In this case, I have only given one example for each turnaround. The rule of thumb is to try and find *at least three examples for each turnaround*.

Let's try that, using the story of the couple who both think the other person doesn't respect them because they understand respect in different ways – one focusing on expressing emotions honestly, and the other focusing on speaking nicely and politely. And let's set it up from her perspective and imagine that she is doing The Work on the belief that 'he doesn't respect me.' She has answered the four questions and has reached the turnarounds. Her task is now to find three examples of each turnaround.

Situation: We are discussing the party next week
Moment: He speaks in a raised voice and uses a swearword
Oneliner: 'He doesn't respect me'

Turnaround: **He *does* respect me**
Example 1: It's not about respect – he's just agitated and raw
Example 2: From his perspective, he is being respectful by being transparent around his emotions
Example 3: He trusts me with his honesty/he doesn't try to protect me

Turnaround: **I don't respect *him***
Example 1: I react from my own biased opinions
Example 2: I don't check in with him before I make up my mind
Example 3: Inside, I attack him for being 'wrong'

Turnaround: **I don't respect *myself***
Example 1: I am creating this story of disrespect myself
Example 2: I ruin a relationship I love by jumping to conclusions
Example 3: I become someone I don't like to be, shutting down my love and becoming hard inside

Find Specific and Genuine Examples *in* the Situation

When you work with the turnarounds, there are a couple of things that can support you in finding good examples:

1. Find examples that are true for you

For the examples to have an effect, they must be *genuine*, by which I mean: they should be examples that are true *for you*. It doesn't matter what everybody else thinks. It's *your* nervous system, and rationalizations and intellectual quibbling won't do any good. You cannot cheat yourself.

2. Find examples in the moment

For the same reason, try to find the examples *in* the specific situation you're working with. I love my son, and 99% of the time, my thoughts around him are positive. But in the moment when he's lying on the sofa, saying, 'why should I?' when I ask him to help lay the table, it's a very different set of thoughts and emotions that fill me. And those are the thoughts I want to work with. It's easy to find examples of how he's supportive in many other situations. The challenge is finding them in *that* specific moment. That's when the beliefs I want to work on are active, so that's the moment in which finding examples can truly shift my thinking.

3. Find specific examples

The more specific you get with your examples, the better. Again: it's all about activating your nervous system to generate simulated experiences. So as an example for a turnaround, you might say: 'I treat him badly.' This is a very general and abstract observation which says nothing about how *specifically* you treat him badly, and as such, does not activate your nervous system to create the felt perception we're looking for. You can move a little closer by specifying that: 'I ignore him.' But to really get in touch with how you're treating him in that moment, you can go all the way to: 'I pretend not to hear it when he asks for the butter.' *This* is being specific. Similarly, 'I don't think he has anything of value to offer,' is a very general observation. 'I reject his input' is better. But: 'I say no to his suggestion about having the meeting on Friday instead' gets you really close to your own behavior and puts you in touch with your example as a specific experience, anchored in the concrete.

What to Remember About Turnaround Examples

Here is what to remember around the examples:

1. Try to find at least 3 examples for each turnaround

2. Find the examples *in* the moment

3. Find examples that are *specific*
   - Concrete actions anchored in a concrete moment

4. Find examples that are *genuine*
   - They must be true for you
   - It doesn't matter what everybody else thinks
   - You cannot cheat yourself

It's all about activating your nervous system, and when you find a good example, it's a good idea to take a moment to pause in the experience, noting how it feels to be present in the situation with this perspective.

If you'd like to see some examples of working with turnarounds, you can turn to *Appendix B: Examples of doing The Work* on page 182 or you can listen to some of the recordings of real sessions of The Work, which you can find links for in *Appendix C: Resources* on page 192. In addition to that, it's best, as always, to just try it out.

Your Turn: Identify the Turnarounds

So now it's your turn to identify the turnarounds in the oneliner you're working with. Write down the oneliner on a piece of paper, and see what turnarounds you can find.

Here is a list of the different variations again:

1. The turnaround to the other
    - Shift people around to get back in your own business. (Note: this turnaround isn't always possible; it requires more than one person to be mentioned in the oneliner.)

2. The turnaround to the self
    - Insert yourself in place of everybody else in the sentence.

3. The turnaround to the opposite
    - Add or remove the word 'not' or find a word that means the opposite.

Go to work!

Only Use First Generation Turnarounds

An important thing to remember when working with the turnarounds is to make sure you never go more than one generation away from the oneliner you're working on.

'He should respect me,' for example, can be turned around like this:

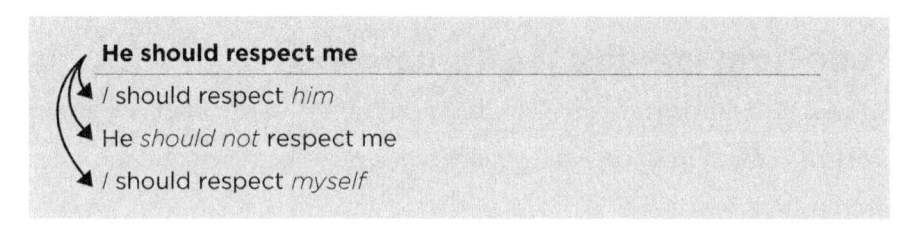

> He should respect me
> - I should respect *him*
> - He *should not* respect me
> - I should respect *myself*

These are all valid turnarounds because they're all direct turnarounds of the oneliner you started with. They're all 'first generation turnarounds.'

What you shouldn't do is this:

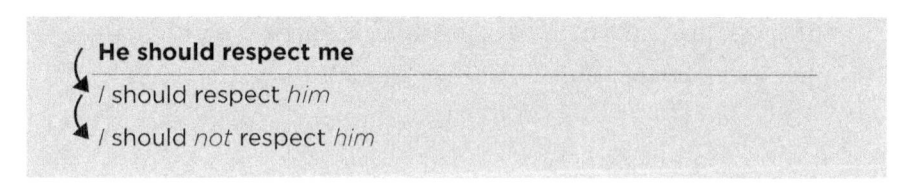

> He should respect me
> - I should respect *him*
> - I should *not* respect *him*

Here, instead of turning around the original oneliner, you have mistakenly turned around the turnaround, doing a turnaround to the other *and* a turnaround to the opposite *simultaneously*. And that's no good. If you start turning around turnarounds, you end up with a version of where you started, in which case, you're no longer finding examples of the opposite of what you believe – you're reinforcing the belief that was causing problems in the first place.

Finding Examples for the Turnarounds

Once you've made sure that all your turnarounds are valid, and you haven't accidentally turned them around twice, it's time to see if you can find at least three examples for each turnaround to show that the turnaround is just as true – or maybe even more true – than the original oneliner.

This can be a tall order. It requires an open mind to find turnaround examples. Since an open mind is one of the effects of doing The Work, however, it gets easier with time, and one of the things you learn is to not only look in the most obvious places for your examples.

Take a situation where you experience that someone is speaking to you in a rude way without you saying anything in return. This could lead to the oneliner: 'John shouldn't speak to me rudely,' and therefore, to the turnaround, '*I* shouldn't speak to *John* rudely.' But here you run aground, because, after all, you didn't say anything.

What if you look below the surface, however? What if you also investigate what's going on *inside* you in the situation? How do you react internally when John speaks to you rudely? Perhaps, as it turns out, you *did* speak to him rudely. You just didn't say anything out loud. Similarly, the oneliner 'I want them to stop being noisy' can end up revealing how noisy *you* are inside your head when you experience someone being noisy around you.

Support Yourself by Taking Your Time in the Four Questions

Another possibility is to pay close attention to what you actually *do* in the situation. If you're working with the oneliner 'I want him to go away,' at some point, you'll come across the turnaround 'I *don't* want him to go away.' And here, you might run aground again, because you do genuinely think that's what you want. But if you investigate how you actually behaved in the situation, it might be that you see something else. You pursued him out into the hallway instead of staying in the room. You kept talking to him, even though he was about to leave. And once he'd gone, you continued the conversation with him in your head for hours.

Your inner images, your inner dialog, your concrete actions, and the ideas you entertain about the past and future in any given situation can contain many examples of the turnarounds you're looking for. Which is one of the reasons why it's a good idea to take your time in answering the first four questions. If you answer them deeply, you will find a lot of material for the turnaround examples there. It's all about becoming still, about delving deeply into yourself and following the mind's associative structures rather than proceeding with strict, mathematical logic.

'I hit him' can just as easily mean that you hit him with your voice. 'I hit myself' can refer to your inner images. Maybe he has only hit you once. How many times have you replayed the movie of that hit in your mind?

Working with the turnarounds is about flow, not force. It's like a stretch in a yoga posture. Avoid putting pressure on yourself. This is a compassionate, inner Inquiry, a gradual opening of your mind, a meditative journey where you gently attempt to prove yourself wrong. And that's a lot to ask. So be patient with yourself. Treat yourself as you would treat a small child learning something new. Your mind will open more and more – and with it, your heart.

Your Turn: Finding Turnaround Examples

Now it's time for you to try and find three examples for each of the turnarounds you have identified.

Remember to find your examples *in* the situation you're working with if you can; be as specific as possible; make sure your examples are genuine to *you*. And remember to give yourself time and be kind to yourself. Finding examples for the turnarounds means asking your mind to look for the complete opposite of what it believes, and that can take some getting used to. We're used to thinking that our survival depends on knowing how our world hangs together, and that our judgments are correct. This is the cause of our pain, but it can take some time to see that, so go easy on yourself.

Go for it!

CHAPTER 10

THE PROCESS AS A WHOLE

Congratulations! You have now done The Work on your first oneliner.

Was it difficult?

People's experiences of starting out on this journey are very varied. Most are a little overwhelmed at first. But don't worry – it quickly becomes a lot easier. As soon as you get a sense of the basic structure, you realize that it's quite simple. Identify a oneliner; answer the four questions; find the turnarounds; and give examples.

It's usually the examples that are the most challenging. This is where the open mind is put to the test. And let me say again: your examples will only have effect if they're genuine. Don't intellectualize and don't try to cheat yourself. It won't work. It's much better to spend twenty minutes finding one good example than to come up with ten examples that are all superficial. You can even take a turnaround with you into your day and keep noticing new examples coming up. Take your time. Be thorough.

And trust!

There are those who find it extremely hard to come up with any examples for the turnarounds in the beginning. If that is the case for you, don't despair. It's similar to physical training. The first mile you run after not having done any exercise for years seems unbearable. If you keep at it, though, you will soon find that what seemed impossible becomes achievable, then manageable, then fine, and eventually, even enjoyable. Have patience with yourself and keep at it, and your mind will open like a flower in spring. I've yet to meet anyone who stayed with the process who didn't experience this transformation.

The Next Step in the Process

Once you've worked the first oneliner on your worksheet, the next step is to do the same with the rest of them, taking each of them through the four questions, the turnarounds, and the examples one by one, until you have been through the whole sheet.

This takes a little time, of course. Depending on how rich the worksheet is and how much time I have available, I usually spend one to two hours on it, going slowly at first, and then picking up speed as I move down the sheet and the situation becomes more and more transparent to me. I often find that when I'm thorough in the beginning, most of the concepts begin to flip around by themselves as it becomes obvious that the turnarounds are way truer than the original beliefs.

I know there are some people who think: one hour – oh my God! I can't spend that much time on a single situation. My suggestion is to simply try it. Test it! Discover for yourself. And to those who think it sounds like a long time to invest in a single worksheet, I can only say: some of these situations have pursued you for years. How much time and negative energy have you already wasted on them? Then imagine going through the rest of your life like that. In my experience, if you go deep in a single worksheet, it can often resolve even the most exhausting problems on the spot. Moreover, it can prevent similar situations arising in the future. If you put the time investment into that context, I'm sure you'll find that it's worth it.

An Experiment

You can do a little experiment: try crossing out the name of the person you wrote your worksheet on and replacing it with that of your mother. Or your partner. Or one of your colleagues. Can you see how the problem is, in reality, not about other people at all? It's actually about you. You're the one carrying it around. And you're the one projecting it onto anybody that happens to fit the profile.

When you work through a worksheet, it's not simply that situation you're working on. It's your map of reality that's changing, and with it, a whole series of other situations in your life – including future ones. When you work through a worksheet, you're putting on shoes instead of trying to tarmac the world. And for each worksheet you work through, your beliefs relax their hold a little more. For each worksheet, it's a little easier to progress. Until one day, an upset man comes bursting into your office and starts telling you off, and the only thing you feel is warmth and understanding.

But that's just my experience. It's of no use to you. You must go through it yourself. And that means doing the whole worksheet. It's not enough to work with a single oneliner every now and then. It can help to relieve an acute attack of panic, worry, or anger, but if you want to uproot the entire network, you need an entire worksheet.

Doing The Work

This is what the process looks like as a whole:

1. Identify the person and the concrete situation causing you emotional stress.

2. Try and find the specific moment in the situation where your emotional reaction was most intense. What was it the other person said or did (or didn't say or do) that got to you?

3. Fill out a 'Judge-Your-Neighbor Worksheet,' remaining in that moment in your inner simulator throughout the process. Remember to use short, simple sentences, and to include the first part of each sentence in points 2 to 6. In point 1, the oneliner is what follows the word 'because.'

4. Start from the top and run each oneliner through the following process:

    a. Answer the four questions, one at a time. (Remember to be present in the moment in your inner simulator, and to answer from there.)

The four questions are:

1. **Is it true?**

    Only answer yes or no. If the answer is no, skip to question 3.

2. **Can you absolutely know that it's true?**

    Only answer yes or no.

3. **How do you react, what happens, when you believe that thought?**

    Be careful not to begin arguing or explaining. Keep an eye out for the word 'because.' Limit yourself to registering *your* responses in the moment.

4. **Who would you be without the thought?**

    Still only in *that* moment.

b. Choose a turnaround and find three examples of how it is just as true (or maybe even more true) in that moment. Make sure that your examples feel true for you. Take the time to experience them inside.

c. When you have come up with three examples, find a new turnaround (being careful not to do 'double turnarounds,' moving more than one generation away) and find three examples of that one, too. Keep going until you can't find any more turnarounds.

5. Move on to the next oneliner on the worksheet and go through points 4a, 4b and 4c, then move to the next oneliner and do the same and continue doing so until you reach point 6 on the worksheet.

6. When you reach point 6 on the worksheet, use the turnarounds specific to this point: 'I am willing to ...' and 'I look forward to ...' Experience them inside.

How to End the Stories that Screw Up Your Life

And so, we arrive at the endpoint. As I wrote at the beginning, there is only now. Everything else is stories – and all your problems are due to these stories. No matter how tempting it might be to think so, reality is never the cause of your problems. Reality simply *is*. And it is only *now*. Problems exist in time and space.

You cannot just decide to change your stories, though. You don't have that much decision-making power. Your stories build on your (perceived) experiences, and only new experiences can change them. Any attempt at force or manipulation is doomed to fail.

There is another way, however.

When you have a problem, it's always because you've locked yourself into a particular position. You're caught in a set of fixed beliefs. But these beliefs are never true. They are interpretations. As self-evident as they may appear, they are only points of view. And when you question them, when you investigate them deeply and put their validity to the test, they dissolve. They have to because no fixed position is ever true. Every time you do an honest Inquiry, you will find that the truth is bigger than you thought.

Faced with the wisdom of your stillness, no fixed position can hold up.

BONUS CHAPTER

FINE-TUNING THE PROCESS

It's a challenging thing to strike the right balance between providing enough information about The Work to allow you to have a real experience of the power of this form of Inquiry, while at the same time, not drowning you in so much detail that you lose your bearings and give up.

What I have shared so far should be enough to put you solidly on track, and yet, there are some further aspects that I know from experience will soon become important for you to be able to continue your explorations and build a proper practice of Inquiry in your life.

The following, therefore, is not meant for your first experiments with The Work – I'm sure you have your hands full with remembering the structure and working with the turnarounds. But once you have found your feet, here are some tips that will support you.

Question 3 in More Depth

Question 3 ('How do you react, what happens, when you believe that thought?') can be difficult to deal with. On the one hand, it can be tempting to slip into stories, explanations, and defensiveness (typically when we say 'because...'); on the other hand, we can find it difficult to move beyond the obvious responses ('I get angry, I raise my voice, I answer in monosyllables'). It can be helpful to have some sub-questions you can ask yourself, to ensure that you have fully explored your reaction (see Figure 6).

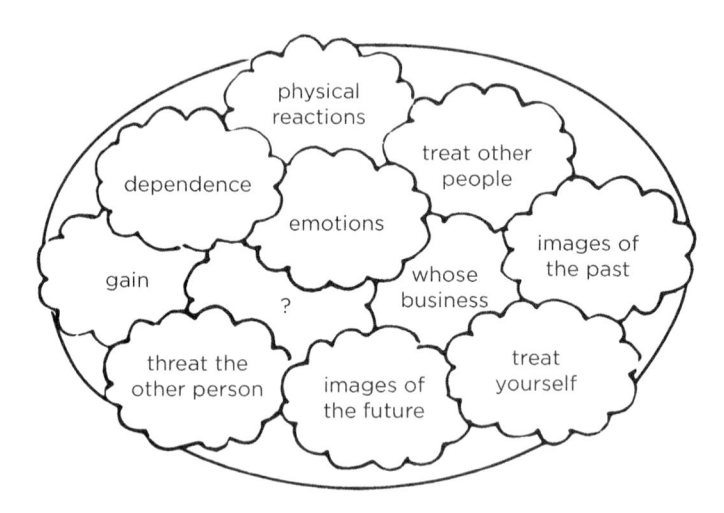

Fig. 5: Sub-questions within question 3
When investigating your reaction in a specific situation, I like to use the image of a house with many different rooms that you can explore one at a time – question 3 being your trip around the house. Or you can use a simpler image, where question 3 is a circle that can be broken down into a series of smaller areas like the one above (physical reactions/emotional responses/" should be: "(physical reactions / emotional responses / inner images etc.), which you can explore with the aid of the sub-questions.

Here is a list of some sub-questions you can pose to further your Inquiry.

Remember that they always pertain to a *specific* moment in a *specific* situation:

- What physical sensations arise when you believe that thought?
- What emotions arise when you believe that thought?
- What are you unable to do when you believe that thought?
- How do you treat yourself when you believe that thought?
- How do you treat other people when you believe that thought?
- What images of the past and future do you see when you believe that thought?
- What obsessions or addictions develop when you believe that thought (alcohol, drugs, credit card, food, sex, TV)?
- What do you think you gain by believing that thought, even though you are not conscious of it?
- Whose business are you in when you believe that thought?

Further Variations on the Worksheet

Just as you can use these sub-questions to deepen your Inquiry in question 3, you can also use the various questions in the 'Judge-Your-Neighbor Worksheet' to cover more ground.

When you filled out your first worksheet, you may have ended up with something like this:

1. **In this situation, who angers, confuses, saddens, or disappoints you, and why?**
   I am angry **with** Peter **because** he doesn't respect me.

2. **In this situation, how do you want them to change? What do you want them to do?**
   I want Peter **to** respect me.

3. **In this situation, what advice would you offer to them?**
   Peter **should** respect me.

4. **In order for you to be happy in this situation, what do you need them to think, say, feel, or do?**
   I need Peter **to** respect me.

5. **What do you think of them in this situation? Make a list.**
   Peter **is** disrespectful.

6. **What is it about this situation that you don't ever want to experience again?**
   I don't ever want to experience Peter being disrespectful to me again.

As you can see, it's quite a short worksheet, and it doesn't offer much insight into what's going on beneath the surface. The main reason for this, of course, is that there is only a single oneliner for each point, but, also, that it is essentially the same oneliner that is being repeated over and over. One thing that can help is to spend a little more time exploring your thoughts in the situation, allowing more space for things to occur to you. But it can also be worthwhile getting a better sense of the difference between the various points on the worksheet.

Let me expand a little on each point to show you what I mean.

How the Points on the Worksheet Differ

Point 1 ('In this situation, who angers, confuses, saddens, or disappoints you, and why?') lays out the framework for the worksheet. This is about identifying the person you're projecting onto, the predominant emotion in the situation, and what exactly it is that is upsetting you in the moment you're working with.

Point 2 ('In this situation, how do you want them to change? What do you want them to do?') contains your childish demands. Here you give yourself permission to be unreasonable. Here you're five years old, throwing a tantrum on the floor. 'I want him to give me the money back.' 'I want him to do as he's told.' 'I want him to apologize.'

Point 3 ('In this situation, what advice would you offer to them?') is your advice for the other person. And here you can help yourself by not just letting it become a continuation of the tantrum in point 2, instead, actually trying to come up with good, useful advice. What concrete things can the other person do to give you what you said you wanted in point 2? Bearing in mind who the other person is, the situation he or she is in, and the limitations of that situation, what would be some good, loving and concrete advice you could offer them? 'He should pause and take a deep breath.' 'He should figure out what he really wants.' 'He should look me in the eye.' 'He should listen to what I'm actually saying.'

Point 4 ('In order for you to be happy in this situation, what do you need them to think, say, feel, or do?') is a list of the things you need to go from the situation described in point 1 to being happy. What do you need the other person to think, say, feel, or do for you to be happy in the moment you're working with? 'I need Peter to say that he has understood me.' 'I need Peter to let me speak.' 'I need Peter to involve me in the decision-making.' The way to tell whether point 4 has been filled out properly is to ask: if I had everything on this list, would I be happy in that moment? And if you realize that something's missing, write it down.

Point 5 ('What do you think of them in this situation? Make a list.') is your judgments of the other person. Here, you're trying to keep yourself to single words and to what you think about him or her in that *exact* moment. You may well think that they're affectionate and caring and sensible at any other point in time – but at *that* moment, when you're gripped by worry or anger or disappointment or jealousy, it's not the kind thoughts that come to the fore. So this is about being honest and getting right down to what you're really thinking, allowing yourself to be petty and judgmental. 'Peter is inconsiderate, mean, self-centered, arrogant, hopeless, incompetent, stupid.'

And point 6 ('What is it about this situation that you don't ever want to experience again') is what you never want to happen again, even if it's a situation that has only arisen once in our life, never to be repeated. What is it you're unwilling to experience a second time? That's what you write for point 6. 'I don't ever want to experience Peter disregarding me like that.' 'I don't ever want to experience him making me feel so insignificant again.'

Working by Yourself or With a Facilitator

Until now, I've only discussed the option of going through the worksheet yourself. It's a good way of doing it, with many practical advantages. Just as you can find the 'Judge-Your-Neighbor Worksheet' online, you can also download a 'One-Belief-at-a-Time Worksheet,' which is designed for exactly that way of working (find out more in *Appendix C: Resources* on page 192). It involves simply taking each oneliner from the 'Judge-Your-Neighbor Worksheet' and transferring it to the 'One-Belief-at-a-Time Worksheet,' which then gives you space both to answer the four questions and to find examples for the turnarounds.

Another way of working is to use a facilitator. This is another person who asks the questions, helps to find turnarounds (not the examples, just the phrases), and supports you so you don't end up telling stories or in some way getting off track. A facilitator can be very useful, especially when you're new to The Work, and there are many different ways of finding one.

You may well already know somebody who is interested in The Work, in which case, you can take turns facilitating each other. But there are also many certified facilitators you can contact. You are welcome to get in touch with me or you can find one via www.thework.com. Another option is to call The Work's free helpline, which has facilitators across the whole world ready to help around the clock. Just as with all the other resources for doing The Work, it is free and completely anonymous– nobody will ask who you are, you don't need to sign up to a newsletter or give your contact details – you can just ring or Skype and get started with The Work straight away. I wholeheartedly recommend it. Having worked on the helpline myself, it's my experience that the people there have no agenda other than to help those who ring up go through their worksheets.

Inquiry is a Practice

When you're in the middle of a strong emotional reaction and your mind is exploding with rage or panic, Inquiry is rarely the best intervention. To do Inquiry, you need to have your deeper mind available, and in those moments, controlling your breathing or counting to ten may be a better option.

When you have calmed down a bit, though, The Work is a great way to investigate what's going on, and inquiring into the painful beliefs that caused the emotions can have a very powerful impact. But the full effect of doing Inquiry does not come from using it as a tool to fix the occasional problem now and then. The full effect comes when you make Inquiry a stable practice.

Set aside some time each week for Inquiry sessions. Just like with yoga or training with an instrument or any other form of meditation, it is the regular practice that makes the difference. Don't wait for the inner pressure to build. Decide on a daily or weekly rhythm that suits you, and be consistent. As you go through your days, take note of situations that bother you or painful thoughts that come up about moments from the past or fears about the future. Fill out a worksheet now and then to capture what's going on while it's fresh in your mind. And when the time comes for your Inquiry session, simply pick one of your worksheets and begin.

I have clients who do this every morning before they start their day and others, who have a couple of evenings each week when they sit down and do The Work. The effects are impressive. When your mind consistently experiences the process of being set free from the illusions of your limiting thoughts, something in you wakes up. As you see through more and more beliefs, you begin to catch up to a reality that is fundamentally kind, uncomplicated and on your side. As this happens, your need to force things subsides and your battle with life quiets down. You become naturally compassionate, honest, direct, connected and full of integrity. Your yeses and nos become clear, choices become simple and you find yourself flooded with joy for no apparent reason.

I sincerely wish you will give yourself this gift. Don't cheat yourself out of the best part!

The journey starts now.

APPENDIX A
WORKSHEET EXAMPLES

What follows is a series of examples of 'Judge-Your-Neighbor Worksheets' filled out by various people in various situations. Notice how each worksheet is anchored in a specific moment and written in short, simple, almost childlike sentences.

THE SITUATION

We're sitting around the table in a restaurant. My dad is sitting beside me. My daughter and her friend are sitting opposite. They want another soft drink, but my dad thinks the soft drinks are too expensive. *The moment that's most painful is just as he says, 'Soft drinks cost an arm and a leg.'*

1. I am embarrassed by my dad because he says that soft drinks cost an arm and a leg.

2. I want my dad to shut up. I want my dad to stop embarrassing me.

3. My dad should put the expense in perspective, be true to his claim that he doesn't worry about money, not be so direct, enjoy this special moment, keep to the plan.

4. I need my dad to offer the children more soft drinks, to pay for the soft drinks without comment, to keep his thoughts to himself, enjoy himself.

5. My dad is stingy, inconsistent, embarrassing, disappointing.

6. I don't ever want to feel embarrassed by my dad again. I don't ever want to experience my dad being stingy again.

THE SITUATION

It's evening. Neil and I are sitting in a cafe, talking. He keeps contradicting me and taking issue with what I say, and I realize that it's because he simply doesn't understand it. *The most painful moment is just as I see his expression when he's looking down at the table (and I realize that he doesn't understand what I'm saying).*

1. I am shocked by Neil because he doesn't understand me.

2. I want Neil to listen to me. I want him to be open to what I'm saying. I want him to understand what I'm saying. I want him to agree with me. I want him to stop being so stubborn. I want him to stop being so persistently stupid. I want him to be the Neil I know. I want him to see that I'm right. I want him to be the person I think he is.

3. Neil should be open toward me. He should listen to me. He should make a bigger effort. He should see that I'm right. He shouldn't fight me on something that's so obviously right. He should consider what I'm saying. He should be still, turn his attention inward and examine himself honestly. He should let go of his intellect. He should

let go of what he knows and look at the world with his own eyes. He should try it. He should listen to what I'm saying instead of just searching for counterarguments.

4. I need Neil to live up to my expectations. I need him to be the person I think he is. I need him to listen. I need him to agree with me. I need him to be on my side. I need him to be someone I can rely on. I need him to respect me.

5. Neil is limited in his intellectual capacity, stubborn, incapable of understanding me. He thinks he's right. He's stupid. He can't see his own limitations. He's much too sure of himself about this.

6. I don't ever want to experience being trapped in this kind of conflict with Neil again. I don't ever want to experience him not being able to see what I see. I don't want to lose him. I don't want to get trapped in a discussion where I can't let go, where I can't just accept that he disagrees.

THE SITUATION

We're in a meeting. Bill asks Maria what she thinks would be the best solution. Maria looks scared and answers tentatively. *The moment I'm working with is just as she says, 'I don't really know ...'*

1. I am annoyed with Maria because she's so unsure of herself.

2. I want Maria to pull herself together. I want Maria to trust herself. I want Maria to speak with authority. I want Maria to dig down inside herself and find her answer.

3. Maria should get still. Make contact with herself. Wait for her response.

4. I need Maria to be more precise. I need Maria to take responsibility for herself. I need Maria to be more self-assured.

5. Maria is weak, a victim, insecure, irritating, easily overwhelmed, fragile.

6. I don't ever want to hear Maria be so tentative again.

THE SITUATION

I'm sitting across from Ann at lunch. She's talking to a friend and I'm trying to start a conversation with them, but she's not interested. *The most painful moment is when she gives me an unenthusiastic smile then turns her attention back to her friend.*

1. I am feeling hurt by Ann, because she isn't giving in to my charm.

2. I want Ann to think I'm special. I want her attention. I want her respect.

3. Ann should notice me. Ann should be interested in me. Ann should see that I'm something special.

4. I need Ann to like me.

5. Ann is reserved and controlled.

6. I don't ever want to feel ignored by Ann again.

THE SITUATION

I'm sitting in my seat in the seminar room. A man comes in and walks around trying to find a place to sit. *The moment irritating me is when I see the conceited way he carries himself.*

1. I am irritated by the man because he thinks he's awesome.

2. I want the man to stop thinking so highly of himself. To understand that we don't care. To behave normally.

3. The man should realize that indulging his ego doesn't help him. Let himself be imperfect. Lose control. Relax. Walk normally. Pay attention to what's actually going on inside him.

4. I need the man to walk normally. Stop trying to attract attention. Disappear.

5. The man is self-centered, attention-hogging, a smart-ass, lost in his ego, unintelligent.

6. I never want to be disturbed by his noisy attention-grabbing attitude again.

THE SITUATION

I'm sitting with Lea in the living room. I've just told her how I'm feeling. She says it sounds like I'm just making it up. *The moment I'm working with is when she says, 'It sounds like you're performing for an audience.'*

1. I am feeling shock and disbelief towards Lea because she is completely misunderstanding what I'm saying.

2. I want her to see me. I want her to understand me. I want her to respect me. I want her to like me. I want her to see the honesty of what I share. I want her to see what I present as genuine.

3. Lea should be more open to what I'm saying. She shouldn't jump to conclusions. She should keep an open mind. She should pay attention to me. She shouldn't let her own beliefs cloud her judgement.

4. I need her to realize that she's got it wrong.

5. Lea is distant, disappointing, wrong.

6. I don't ever want Lea to not respect me again. I don't ever want to be misunderstood by Lea again.

THE SITUATION

We're sitting around the table at the department meeting.

Louise has just set out her plan. I ask a question, and she begins her response with, 'Yes, as I've just explained ...' *That is the moment that hurts the most.*

1. I am defensive towards Louise because she thinks my question is stupid.

2. I want Louise to say it's an excellent question. I want Louise to answer my question. I want Louise to stop criticizing me. I want Louise to appreciate my question. I want Louise to make me feel okay about asking. I want Louise to take the time to give me a serious answer. I want Louise to not blow me off.

3. Louise should listen more attentively to what I'm asking. She shouldn't criticize me in front of the others. She should take me more seriously.

4. I need Louise to love me. I need Louise to think that I've done nothing wrong. I need Louise to understand why I'm asking. I need Louise to make me feel good about asking. I need her to let me know it's ok.

5. Louise is harsh, judgmental, doesn't say what she really means, critical, an authority, disappointing.

6. I don't ever want to be criticized by Louise again. I don't ever want to feel that Louise thinks I've done something wrong. I don't ever want to experience Louise making me feel guilty and ashamed.

THE SITUATION

I'm sixteen years old. I'm standing in my room with my mother, looking at myself in the mirror. *My mother says, 'Look at how fat you are!'*

1. I am feeling devastated by my mother because she's insulting me.

2. I want her to stop telling me that I look terrible, I want her to stop telling me that there is something wrong with me. I want her to stop criticizing me, to back off, to leave the room. I want her to stop hurting me.

3. My mother should take a deep breath, she should look at me, she should see how hurt I am by her words, she should recognize that the way she speaks to me is not helpful, she should remember my efforts to lose weight, she should speak kindly to me, she should tell me that she wants to help me.

4. I need my mother to be kind to me, to be my friend, to sit with me, to help me find a solution, to be on my side, to acknowledge me, to show me that she cares for me.

5. My mother is insulting, cruel, unconscious, sharp, hurtful, criticizing, aggressive, attacking, panicking, helpless, devastating, inconsiderate, not a proper mother.

6. I don't ever want to experience being devastated by my mother again.

THE SITUATION

I'm seven years old and being looked after by my aunt and uncle. I'm playing with the curtains in their living room. When my aunt comes downstairs and sees me, she says in a tired way that I'm not allowed to mess around with the curtains. *The painful moment is when I hear the tired/dismissive tone of her voice.*

1. I am feeling completely in the wrong because my aunt thinks I'm irritating.

2. I want my aunt to give me permission to be who I am. I want her to love me as I am. I don't want her to always think I'm doing something wrong.

3. She should be more open, more curious, more accommodating. She shouldn't judge me, shouldn't be so judgmental. She should see that I'm doing my best. She should remember that I don't know their rules and routines.

4. I need her to show me she thinks I'm ok. I need her to be more open toward me.

5. My aunt is narrow-minded, insensitive, restricted, out of touch with her feelings, doesn't understand children.

6. I don't ever want to feel that I'm the one who needs to change because my aunt doesn't get me.

APPENDIX B
EXAMPLES OF DOING THE WORK

The following are some selected examples of how various people have done The Work. I have used only a single oneliner from each worksheet, paring the process down to the key points.

1. He doesn't care about me

The situation: I'm sitting in a café, waiting for Andreas, when I get a text from him saying that he's going to be fifteen minutes late.
The moment: Just as I read the text
The belief: Andreas doesn't care about me

1. Is it true that Andreas doesn't care about you?
Yes.

2. Can you absolutely know that Andreas doesn't care about you?
No.

3. How do you react, what happens, when you believe the thought that he doesn't care about you?
I get annoyed. I get a burning sensation in my stomach. My arms and hands tense up. I feel ignored, insignificant. I see an image of Andreas chatting with somebody, completely indifferent to the fact that I'm waiting. I see images of situations from our past when Andreas has been uncaring toward me. I see images from my future where he keeps letting me down. My forehead feels tense. I can feel a furrow between

my brows. It feels like I've been punched in the stomach. I feel heavy. I'm sad. I have a lump in my throat. I feel small. I see images of situations from my childhood where people disregarded me: the schoolyard, scouts. I attack myself: I'm not interesting enough to talk to. My back slumps. I see myself as I imagine he sees me. Everything goes gray. I wince. My body contracts. My breathing is shallow. I feel in pain. I get angry. I attack Andreas in my mind: who does he think he is? I compare our lives, looking for proof that I'm better than him. I see images from situations where he told me about problems with his girlfriend. I see images from situations where he complained about his job. I feel superior to him. I feel better than him. I create distance between us. I feel more grown-up than him. I fully enter into this well-known feeling of being 'more grown-up.' I feel better than the other people in the café. I feel solitary. Nobody understands me. I'm completely alone. I start to feel insecure. I lose a sense of connection to my surroundings. I'm superior to the world. I look at Andreas with forbearance. I feel distant from him. I see myself greeting him when he comes without mentioning his lateness. I see him being apologetic, while I act like nothing happened. I feel far away. I feel upset.

4. Who would you be without the thought that he doesn't care about you?

Calm. Relaxed. At ease. I'm enjoying my tea. I feel the sunlight warming my face. I feel peaceful. I'm looking forward to seeing him. I'm enjoying this unexpected pause. I'm grateful that he's on his way. I feel connected to myself. I'm present in the here and now. I can feel my breath. I can hear the sounds around me. I'm happy.

Turnaround 1: Andreas does care about me

a. He's sent me a text.
b. His lateness has nothing to do with me / it's not personal.
c. He's on his way to meet me.

Turnaround 2: I don't care about Andreas

a. I'm not interested in why he's late.
b. I'm not interested in his needs – I just want him to attend to mine.
c. I don't feel forgiving toward him when I'm trapped in this thought. I treat him badly.

Turnaround 3: I don't care about myself

a. I let this story develop without checking in with myself and exploring what's really going on inside me.
b. I'm wasting my time being annoyed instead of enjoying the pause in my day.
c. I have lost a friend in that moment, and I'm the one who threw him out, without considering that I want him as a friend.

2. My mother finds fault with my work

The situation: My mother is visiting. I've just put up new wallpaper in the kitchen, and I show her. The first thing she says is: 'Did you notice there's a flaw in the paper?'
The moment: When she says, 'Did you notice there's a flaw in the paper?'
The belief: My mother finds fault with my work.

1. Is it true that your mother finds fault with your work?
Yes.

2. Can you absolutely know that your mother finds fault with your work?
Yes.

3. How do you react, what happens, when you believe the thought that your mother finds fault with your work?
I feel terrible. There's a flaw right in the middle of it. It's ruined. I lose all pleasure in what I've done. I'm not proud of it anymore. It feels like everything's been torn to pieces. Like I need to start from scratch. It was so beautiful, but now it's just crap. She's ruined it. Now I can't help seeing it. How could I have overlooked it? I feel winded. It's like she's hit me. It's not special anymore. There's a flaw right in the middle. She's taken all the joy out of it. I see images of myself at art school, with my teacher being similarly critical. Just picking the whole thing apart when I bring it out. I see images of my mother when I was little, how she did the same thing when I brought a sculpture home from school, saying, 'You're not bringing that inside the house!' I treat her as if she's the final authority. As if her opinion is the only one that matters. As if she can control how I feel. As if she's the one with the power to destroy things or build them up. I attack myself. I'm so stupid – how could I not have seen that? I get tough and critical toward myself. 'Don't you know how to do that kind of stuff by now?' I don't feel as if I have the right to be proud of what I've done. I can't hear that my mother's just making an observation. I can't hear anything other than her criticizing me. I just see her as hypercritical and irritating. I don't want to listen to her. I want her out of the kitchen.

4. Who would you be without the thought that she's finding fault with your work?

It feels completely different. I'm not thinking in terms of mistakes anymore. I'm not agitated or upset at all. I just hear it as information: 'Look, there's a little flaw in the paper there.' It's just a little thing. It's so small. Without the thought I'm just impressed by my mother: wow, she's really sharp. And that's not a problem. It's just something we have together, it's not destroying anything. I don't think other people will notice it. It's incredible that she saw it. I'm just impressed by her. I lose none of my enthusiasm. I still feel very happy with what I've done. I just find it amusing. It feels nice. Without the thought, I stay in the place where I'm pleased with my efforts. And grateful, actually, because she saw it. I feel connected to her. I feel closer to myself.

Turnaround 1: I find fault with my work

a. The moment she points it out, I tear it to pieces. I'm not enjoying it any longer. I can only see that it's all wrong.
b. I attack myself: 'You should have checked the paper, you should have done a proper job, you should have gone about it differently.' There's a long list of things I think I should have done differently.
c. I tell myself I'm stupid. That my mother is better at it than I am.

Turnaround 2: I find fault with her work

a. I grumble about her in my head.
b. I think she should have said something positive first.
c. I don't think she should point out the one thing that's wrong.

Turnaround 3: My mother isn't finding fault with my work

a. It was a flaw in the paper – it wasn't my work she was criticizing.

b. It was the only negative thing she said. She didn't look for flaws anywhere else.

c. In reality, it wasn't actually a flaw – what does that even mean? It was just how the paper was.

3. He's rejecting me

The situation: It's evening. I'm lying in bed with my husband. I want to have sex with him and stroke his back, but he pulls the duvet up around him and says, 'I'm too tired.'

The moment: When he says, 'I'm too tired.'

Belief: He's rejecting me

1. Is it true that he's rejecting you?
Yes.

2. Can you absolutely know that it's true that he's rejecting you?
No.

3. How do you react, what happens, when you believe the thought that he's rejecting you?
I feel unhappy. I get the wind knocked out of my sails. I'm disappointed. I pull back my hand. I curl up. Everything goes rigid inside. My breathing is shallow. I shut him out, retreating completely into myself. I become still. I put a wall up between us. I feel abandoned. I feel rejected. I think there's something wrong with me. I feel unlovable. I see all my flaws: I'm too old, my body isn't attractive. I see images of other (younger) women and compare myself with them. I compare myself with Annabeth from

his office. I count how long it's been since we last had sex. I blame myself for not exercising enough. I feel like a victim. I'm too busy. I see images of other situations where I feel he's rejected me. I see him as distant, uninterested, cold. I wonder whether our marriage will last. I think about our trip to a restaurant last week, when he sat there with his mobile. I get angry with him. He should prioritize me more. He works too much. I think he's unreasonable. I can't love him. I don't feel any understanding for him at all. I attack him. I think there's something wrong with him. I look down on him. I wonder whether I'm with the right person. I think of other men I know who I think are interested in me. I see images of what my life would be like with somebody else. I feel uneasy. I get a sinking feeling in my stomach. I'm afraid I've made the wrong choice. That I'm missing out on something important. I feel trapped. I tear our marriage to shreds. I get divorced in that moment. I can only see what's wrong with him. I get annoyed by his breathing. I feel completely alone in the world.

4. Who would you be without the thought that he's rejecting you?
Without the thought, all my affection returns. I feel great tenderness toward him. I can see how hard he's working right now. I would let my hand lie there. I would kiss him. I would tell him it's fine. I would be happy with our marriage. I would feel secure. I feel close to him. My stomach is unclenched, my body relaxed. I feel the bed and the duvet. My breathing is peaceful. I feel centered. I love him.

Turnaround 1: He isn't rejecting me
a. He says he's too tired, not that there's something wrong with me.
b. He can't control what he's in the mood for.
c. He respects me enough to be honest and is confident I can cope.

Turnaround 2: I'm rejecting him

a. I move my hand.
b. I'm giving him the silent treatment.
c. I turn away from him.
d. I attack him in my mind.

Turnaround 3: I'm rejecting myself

a. I'm the one creating the story that he's rejecting me (instead of just hearing that he's too tired).
b. I'm attacking myself for not being good enough. I'm telling myself that the life I've chosen is the wrong one.
c. I clamp down on my affection / reject the side of myself that loves him.

4. Albert isn't helping me

The situation: I'm doing The Work and Albert is facilitating me. I've fallen into a long silence and don't know what to do, but Albert doesn't do anything to help me move forward.
The moment: I'm sitting there in silence, feeling disheartened.
Belief: Albert isn't helping me

1. Is it true that Albert isn't helping you?
Yes.

2. Can you absolutely know that it's true that Albert isn't helping you?
Yes.

3. How do you react, what happens, when you believe the thought that Albert isn't helping you?

I feel alone. I feel judged. I get confused. I don't know what to do. I'm pulled out of The Work. I can't concentrate. I feel stupid. I treat myself as if I'm stupid. I tell myself to pull myself together, that I'm about to ruin everything. I attack myself. I treat Albert like an enemy. I want to get out of here. I don't want to be here anymore. I feel like he's abandoned me. In my mind I see him roll his eyes impatiently. I treat him as if he's an authority figure. I have no respect for him in that moment. I'm afraid of him. I'm also angry with him. Angry that he's letting me struggle on alone like that. I feel pressure behind my eyes, my jaw clenches, my face crumples, I feel empty inside, as if there's a void in my stomach. I'm sad. I can't manage this by myself! I feel helpless, like a victim. I want to cry. I've got completely stuck, and I have no idea how to move forward. I feel dependent on Albert. I'm angry because he's not trying to help me. At the same time, I'm annoyed with myself because I can't figure out how to continue without help.

4. Who would you be without the thought that Albert isn't helping you?

I relax. I stay focused. I'm connected with my Work. I trust myself and the process. There's a great sense of stillness inside me. I trust that something will come up if I just remain in this stillness. I feel calm. Connected. It feels like Albert and I are creating this stillness together. He's giving me time and space. I'm peaceful, attentive. My confidence that something will come up is now so great that I could remain in this stillness forever. I feel completely filled by it. Strong. My awareness that Albert is there increases my attentiveness and the stillness inside me. It feels very strong.

Turnaround 1: Albert is helping me

a. By being quiet, so I can sink deeper within myself.

b. By showing confidence that something will turn up.

c. By simply waiting for me to say something.

Turnaround 2: I'm not helping myself

a. By withdrawing from the process, by not having confidence in it.

b. By doing myself down instead of giving myself what I need.

c. By creating stories about Albert, by being in his business.

Turnaround 3: I'm not helping Albert

a. By seeing him as an enemy.

b. By withdrawing from The Work.

c. By not telling Albert what's going on – by thinking he should be able to read my mind.

APPENDIX C
RESOURCES

I have prepared a ton of resources to support you on your journey with Inquiry. They come free with this book, and you can download them on **www.theartofbeinghuman.com/endthestories.**

Here is what you can find:

- ✓ Links to the Judge-Your-Neighbor Worksheet for download (also included on the next page)

- ✓ Links to the One-Belief-at-a-Time Worksheet for download

- ✓ Links to The Work App on Apple's Appstore or Google Play

- ✓ My Facilitation Guide for download

- ✓ A series of podcasts on how to do The Work, including:
  - A guided meditation supporting you to fill out a Judge-Your-Neighbor Worksheet
  - Real-life recordings of people actually doing The Work

- ✓ Easy to follow video presentations with instructions on how to do The Work

- ✓ A Q&A section where I will answer any question you have around Inquiry.

- ✓ Information about online courses and other activities to support you in learning how to do Inquiry

Simply go to www.theartofbeinghuman.com/endthestories to find all these materials (and more) waiting for you!

Byron Katie's Books and Website

Byron Katie has written several books on The Work. I recommend two in particular:

- *Loving What Is*
- *I Need Your Love, Is It True?*

Byron Katie's website for The Work at www.thework.com is a treasure trove of resources as well. Here you can find:

- ✓ The Helpline for The Work
- ✓ Lists of Certified Facilitators in your area
- ✓ Materials for doing The Work
- ✓ Links to YouTube videos with Katie doing The Work
- ✓ Information about Katie's events and activities

(Ernest's)
Facilitation Guide
for The Work of Byron Katie

Choose the one-liner you want to work with. Invite the client to become mentally and emotionally present in the situation where he or she believed the thought. Give the client time to become still and experience their answer. The Work is a meditation. Give them space.

1. Is it true?
Here you can only answer 'yes' or 'no'. If the answer is 'no', move straight to question 3.

2. Can you absolutely know that it's true?
Here, again, you can only answer 'yes' or 'no'.

3. How do you react, what happens, when you believe that thought?
Let the client answer this question freely, and if it feels right, if you want to, and if time allows, you could use some of these sub-questions:

- What physical sensations arise when you believe that thought?
- What emotions arise when you believe that thought?
- How do you treat the other person when you believe that thought?
- How do you treat yourself when you believe that thought?
- What are you unable to do, when you believe that thought?"
- What images of the past and future do you see when you believe that thought?
- What obsessions or addictions develop when you believe that thought (alcohol, drugs, credit card, food, sex, TV)?
- What do you think you gain by believing that thought, even if you're not conscious of it?
- Whose business are you in when you believe that thought?

4. Who would you be without the thought?
Who would you be in the situation if you were unable to believe that thought?

Turn the thought around
Ask the client to suggest a turnaround themselves. Check that it's valid (see below) and ask them to come up with a genuine, specific example that demonstrates how the turnaround is just as true – or maybe even more true – than the original belief. See if you can get your client to find three examples for each turnaround. If the client can't find a turnaround, suggest one.

Here are some examples of turnarounds:

Original sentence:	I want Laura to respect me
Swap round the people:	I *want me* to respect *Laura*
Insert yourself in every place:	I want *me* to respect *myself*
Add or remove 'not':	I *don't* want Laura to Respect me
Replace with opposite word:	I want Laura to *disrespect* me

The Work is © by Byron Katie International, Inc - www.thework.com
This Facilitation Guide is © by www.theartofbeinghuman.com

(Ernest's)
Facilitation Guide
for The Work of Byron Katie

The role of the facilitator
There is nothing complicated about being a facilitator. There's nothing you need to understand, do or figure out. You just need to ask the questions in whatever way comes naturally to you, and then give the client space to find their own answers. You're not there to give advice; you're not there to be sympathetic, express agreement or disagreement or involve yourself in the client's answers in any other way. You're just there to ask the questions and let the client answer.

The role of the client
The Work is an exploration and a meditation. It's about attentiveness; it's not about forcing yourself to change your mind. Listen to the question, let your mind become still and be open to the answers that appear. Be careful not to lose yourself in stories, explanations or arguments. The moment you stop answering the questions, The Work stops working.

Asking the questions
It's a good idea to repeat the one-liner at regular intervals to keep the client on track. Instead of simply asking, 'Is it true?' you can ask, *'Ben never cleans up after himself* – is it true?' or 'How do you react, what happens, when you believe the thought that *Ben never cleans up after himself*'?

Remain in the situation
As far as possible, support the client to answer and give examples from the concrete situation he or she has identified. It's fine to come up with examples from other areas of life, but it's best if the client can describe their reactions (questions 3 and 4) and find examples of turnarounds in the concrete situation he or she is working with.

Avoid losing yourself in stories
It can be tempting for the client to go off on a tangent and begin to argue, give background details or lose themselves in stories that lead them away from the situation and the inquiry. As the facilitator, you can listen out for the words 'because' and 'but', which often reveal that the client is getting off track. If that happens, gently guide the client back by asking the question again.

Investigating through the senses
When, as a client, you experience or re-experience reactions, emotions and situations, there's a big difference between 'thinking about them' and 'perceiving them through your senses'. See whether you can experience them with your whole sensory apparatus. Take your time, closing your eyes if you find it helpful, and immerse yourself in the experience. The more of 'yourself' you can transport back to the experience, the stronger the reactions in your nervous system will be, and the easier it is to do The Work.

The Work is © by Byron Katie International, Inc - www.thework.com
This Facilitation Guide is © by www.theartofbeinghuman.com

THE WORK OF BYRON KATIE — Judge-Your-Neighbor Worksheet

Judge your neighbor • Write it down • Ask four questions • Turn it around

Think of a recurring stressful situation, a situation that is reliably stressful even though it may have happened only once and recurs only in your mind. As you answer each of the questions below, allow yourself to mentally revisit the time and place of the stressful occurrence. Use short, simple sentences.

1. In this situation, who angers, confuses, saddens, or disappoints you, and why?

   I am _____ with _____ because _____
         emotion   *name*

   Example: I am angry with Paul because he doesn't listen to me.

2. In this situation, how do you want them to change? What do you want them to do?

   I want _____ to _____
         name

   Example: I want Paul to see that he is wrong. I want him to stop lying to me. I want him to see that he is killing himself.

3. In this situation, what advice would you offer to them?

   _____ should/shouldn't _____
      name

   Example: Paul should take a deep breath. He should calm down. He should see that his behavior frightens me. He should know that being right is not worth another heart attack.

4. In order for *you* to be happy in this situation, what do you need them to think, say, feel, or do?

   I need _____ to _____
         name

   Example: I need Paul to hear me when I talk to him. I need him to take care of himself. I need him to admit that I am right.

5. What do you think of them in this situation? Make a list. (Remember, be petty and judgmental.)

   _____ is _____
      name

   Example: Paul is unfair, arrogant, loud, dishonest, way out of line, and unconscious.

6. What is it about this situation that you don't ever want to experience again?

   I don't ever want _____

   Example: I don't ever want Paul to lie to me again. I don't ever want to see him ruining his health again.

Now investigate each of the above statements using the four questions. Always give yourself time to let the deeper answers meet the questions. Then turn each thought around. For the turnaround to statement 6, replace the words "I don't ever want to..." with "I am willing to..." and "I look forward to..." Until you can look forward to all aspects of life without fear, your Work is not done.

The four questions

Example: Paul doesn't listen to me.

1. Is it true? (Yes or no. If no, move to 3.)
2. Can you absolutely know that it's true? (Yes or no.)
3. How do you react, what happens, when you believe that thought?
4. Who would you be without the thought?

Turn the thought around

a) to the self. (*I don't listen to myself.*)
b) to the other. (*I don't listen to Paul.*)
c) to the opposite. (*Paul does listen to me.*)

Then find at least three specific, genuine examples of how each turnaround is true for you in this situation.

For more information on how to do The Work, visit thework.com

ACKNOWLEDGEMENTS

There are so many people to thank for the existence of this book.

I used to find it corny when authors thanked their clients and participants in their books, but I must say, it makes complete sense to me today. I owe so much to all those who have trusted me with their honesty, their pain, and their vulnerability over the years, and who have taught me such valuable lessons about myself and what it means to be human.

I am also deeply grateful to Byron Katie whose razor-sharp love and deep dedication to sharing the process of The Work is, in my opinion, among the greatest gifts on our planet at the moment. She stands with countless others who have been kind enough to share their findings, experiences, and insights in the age-old tradition of passing on the wisdom. If it wasn't for their generosity, we would be fumbling in the dark for answers that we can now find with a quick search on the internet.

I've had the joy of getting feedback from many people during the writing process, and I'm very grateful to all of you. In particular, I want to mention Annette Birkmann, whose comments are always precise and encouraging, and Liat Gat, who appeared out of nowhere with so many kind and useful suggestions.

Over the years, I've worked with many great and inspiring people, and through our shared practices, I've learned so much about Inquiry. In particular, I want to thank Nora Perry, Sarah-Maya Côté Jirik, Tom Compton and Ursula Carlin for their friendship and support. What a journey we're on!

And finally, I'm grateful to Charlotte Rosenberg for her illustrations, Mette Damgaard for her support, Ida Fia Sveningsson for designing the book, and Lise Cartwright and Chandler Bolt for help with the process of publishing and divining the mysterious workings of the Amazon website!

SHARE THE LOVE

Reviews on Amazon are crucial to helping others find great books to read and consequently to the success of this one as well.

If you've enjoyed reading *How to End the Stories that Screw Up Your Life* you would do me a huge favor by going to the Amazon website to leave a brief, honest review. You can make it as long as you like, of course, but it doesn't have to be more than a single line to have an impact.

The ripple effect of even the smallest action can change the world!

Share the love.

Printed in Great Britain
by Amazon